Policy and Rights Challenges in Children's Online Behaviour and Safety, 2017–2023

Andy Phippen

Policy and Rights Challenges in Children's Online Behaviour and Safety, 2017–2023

Second Edition 2025

palgrave
macmillan

Andy Phippen
Bournemouth University
Poole, UK

ISBN 978-3-031-80285-0 ISBN 978-3-031-80286-7 (eBook)
https://doi.org/10.1007/978-3-031-80286-7

This Palgrave Macmillan imprint is published by the registered company Springer Nature Switzerland AG.
The registered company address is: Gewerbestrasse 11, 6330 Cham, Switzerland

If disposing of this product, please recycle the paper.

CONTENTS

LIST OF FIGURES

LIST OF TABLES

CHAPTER 1

Online Safety Policy—Moving On?

Abstract This book examines the evolution of online safety policy for children in the UK and beyond, analysing shifts in legislative efforts from 2017 to 2023, including the enactment of the UK Online Safety Act 2023. Building on prior work, we explore the concept of an online safeguarding dystopia, where well-meaning but restrictive policies limit children's rights under the guise of protection. By applying Bronfenbrenner's ecological systems theory, the text dissects the "online safety ecosystem", which involves various stakeholders—from policy makers to educators and families—who impact children's online experiences. The book critiques a dominant reliance on technological and punitive measures, arguing that such approaches ignore the complex, contextual nature of children's lives and often fail to align with youth voices. It highlights a disconnection between policies intended to keep children safe and the practical realities they face. Ultimately, the author calls for an evidence-based, multi-stakeholder approach to online safety, one that embraces empowerment, education, and a nuanced understanding of the risks children face, to foster a digital environment that genuinely serves their best interests.

Keywords Online safety policy • Child rights • Ecological systems theory • Safeguarding dystopia • Stakeholder collaboration

© The Author(s), under exclusive license to Springer Nature Switzerland AG 2025
A. Phippen, *Policy and Rights Challenges in Children's Online Behaviour and Safety, 2017–2023*,
https://doi.org/10.1007/978-3-031-80286-7_1

1

It's better just to ignore what adults tell you. Young person, 17, 2021.

This book is the follow-up to a previous monograph *Children's Online Behaviour and Safety—Policy and Rights Challenges*, which was published in 2017 (Phippen, 2017) and considered Online Safety Policy and Practice between 2010 and 2016. In that book the prevailing narrative was one of using technology to prevent young people from being exposed to harms, regardless of the impact of these approaches upon their rights. In developing these arguments, I proposed the concept of the *online safeguarding dystopia* where, in our rush to ensure young people were protected from harm online (without ever comprehensively defining what these harms were), we have eroded their rights and ignored their wishes because we (adults) know best and we will make sure they are safe.

This book will follow similar format to the previous one but is completely new content considering the state of the online safety policy field in the UK (and more broadly) from 2017 to 2023 but will extend the concept of the dystopia to look more broadly at what we have come to refer to as the *online safety ecosystem*, a model comprising all stakeholders who should have a responsibility for child safeguarding. That is not to say that the dystopia has improved since the last book, more that it has evolved, as we will explore in this book.

While there is growing body of knowledge related to child online safety, and certainly a lot of media and policy interest, there still remain only a small number of authors compared to other areas of social policy and most will focus on behaviours and not more broadly at the policy space, with analysis of rhetoric, evidence and WHY public policy has evolved in tension with the needs of those it claims to protect.

This book attempts to unpick this tension based on almost twenty years of empirical work across the stakeholder space and, most importantly, conversations with many young people. In trying to understand why we are where we currently are, it will attempt to explain why there are better, more child-centric approaches and why existing approaches are doomed to fail because they ignore history.

In terms of policy development, the period of study for this edition starts with examination of the emergence and failures of the child safety aspects of the Digital Economy Act 2017, and the moves to explore development of the Online Safety Act 2023 2023 and its assent. However, it is also considering digital aspects of education statutory instruments and other legislation with digital elements. All of this is considered against a backdrop of youth voice and evidence from the field.

While the focus lies in UK policy, it will also draw upon similar policies in other parts of the world and the move from a starting place of multi-stakeholder engagement to the current established practice of platform liability and, arguably, industry scapegoating. The book will draw on significant data sources to illustrate the grassroots need compared to policy direction and political and media rhetoric as well as considerable ethnographic reflection from someone who has been engaged across the stakeholder space in the field for twenty years.

STUDYING THE ONLINE SAFETY SPACE

My own work in this area (Lacohee et al., 2006) started somewhat by accident. During a project with a couple of industry service providers exploring public trust and engagement with online systems in the early twenty-first century, we decided that it might be interesting to speak to some young people about their experiences with online systems. Sat in a school, we had organized two focus groups with year 10 students (aged between 14 and 15). The school was very supportive—they had noticed that more and more young people were talking about doing things online, yet they had little understanding of these issues and wanted to learn more. The young people were firstly surprised "adults" wanted to talk to them about these sorts of things, but soon warmed up and we spent far longer than planned talking to them. "This is better than being in class", one of them said. In those conversations we experienced young people who were very engaged with online service (like MSN, Bebo, and MySpace) and who gained a lot of enjoyment from interacting with others on these platforms. However, when we asked them about the concerns that were emerging in the media about grooming and what was still referred to then as "stranger danger", some of them did acknowledge sometimes you did get approached by strangers who would ask strange things. "It's ok though", we were told, "they just pervs and we block them". What became clear was that, with a dearth of adult intervention and, arguably, interest, they had built their own support networks among peers, and made use of the tools provided by platforms to manage their own safety. They were knowledgeable about the potential harms and were more concerned with arguments among peers than being groomed by strangers, and generally enjoyed their online interactions.

The school asked if we might do some more sessions, and around the same time I was introduced to a charity who provided broadband for schools but were increasingly giving advice on online safety issues to their customers. This led to the means to collect data on a larger scale (given the number of schools they supported) and access to other stakeholders, such as politicians and civil servants, who were also tackling this burgeoning area of social policy. I was invited to give talks and staff training in schools and across the wider children's workforce, and national speaking invitations lead to more interaction in the policy space and industry. The charity developed new tools for schools to use to manage their online safety, and I was asked to look at the data they collected from these tools, and as interest in online safety globally grew, so did my interactions in the ecosystem. However, what remained at its core were interactions with young people and, to this day, speaking to young people is always the most enlightening, interesting and impactful use of my research time.

However, something does trouble me. In these early days when I first spoke with young people about their online lives, one question I would ask is, "What can adults do to help". I was told that adults need to stop freaking out, to listen to their concerns, and not tell them things like "you shouldn't be doing that". Essentially, they wanted non-judgemental support and help in the rare event that something upsetting might happen. However, most doubted that would happen so, instead, they turned to peers for support.

And when I speak to young people twenty years later, they say the same thing.

Which makes me wonder whether all this work has been worth it! However, I will press on, and continue to listen to young people.

In this book I attempt to understand why things seem to be staying the same (or, as we will see in Chap. 5, sometimes getting worse). Certainly, at a personal level there is something extremely frustrating in seeing young people call for change, only to be told that is not the change they need and adults have better answers.

I would, broadly, describe myself as an ethnographer of online safety. And I am mindful that I am not simply an observer in this context, I am also a stakeholder, with the means to reach policy makers and try to inform what they do at a macro level, but also communicate to those stakeholders closer to the child about what they do and how they can best be supported.

Ethnography has a well-established foothold in social sciences to study and understand human cultures, communities, and social practices.

Broadly, it aims to provide a detailed, in-depth description of the everyday life and practices of a particular group of people from an insider's perspective and the methodological approach immersing oneself in the daily lives of the people being studied, participating in their activities, and observing their behaviours and interactions.

And this is what I try to do, to understand what young people do online and the potential harms they might encounter, to understand how they build resilience and interact with stakeholders in their safety around them, and to understand the distance in the ecosystem between what young people are asking for, and what policy makers implement. And perhaps most challenging, I try to understand why policy makers keep doing the things they do.

More specifically, I try to bring a rational, evidence led exploration of the online safety ecosystem. I try to avoid saying "I think that...", and instead only put forward suggestions informed by evidence and data. And that data comes from a wide variety of sources, and I have, over the years, worked with young people, schools, children's workforce, industry, NGOs, media, regulators and policy makers in the UK and internationally. The nature of data collected from those interactions (that might be discussions, round tables, presentations, conversations, or more formal interviews) is generally observational and anecdotal (as any reader of this book will discover) but also comes from extremely large datasets (discussed mainly in Chaps. 4 and 5 but also via anecdotes throughout this book) that result from work with NGOs and schools and provide a significant source of evidence in tension with policy direction.

But with all these interactions, I am always focussed on whether whatever is occurring makes a positive contribution to what young people have, for many years, told us they want, or whether there are other agendas at play.

Understanding the Online Safety Ecosytem

During time conducting research across the online safety space, I have worked extensively with Prof Emma Bond. Starting from a similar point of discussing issues with young people, we soon discovered we were doing similar work in different parts of the country and started to collaborate. Over the years this collaboration has resulted in many outputs related to online safety (e.g. Phippen & Bond, 2022, 2023). During the development of this work, we recognized how important a model to highlight the various stakeholders in online safety would be and set about developing one. It has become the theoretical foundation with which we now explore the online safety policy area, and helps us to understand why it continues to fail.

Using Bronfenbrenner's (1979) Ecology of Child Development as a starting point, this ecosystem model is now used extensively in our work, especially with policy makers, to understand the need for multi-stakeholder approaches. It has appeared in many peer-reviewed outputs (e.g. Phippen & Bond, 2002, 2023) but I will reproduce it here because it is the foundation upon which I will deconstruct policy in alignment with the stakeholders around the child, and the young people themselves.

Bronfenbrenner's seminal work integrates both nature and nurture perspectives, emphasizing that a child's development is influenced not only by their biology but also by their interactions with other actors in their environment, such as family, community, and society. Actions within any of these actors can impact the wider ecosystem of development. Thus, to provide the most effective context for child development, we must consider both the child and their environment, and the interactions between those with responsibilities for the child's protection and safety. Within his ecosystem model, Bronfenbrenner defined several different systems around the child:

- Macrosystem: the broad cultural, societal, and institutional influences that shape an individual's development. This outermost layer encompasses the overarching beliefs, values, customs, and laws of the society in which a person lives, affecting all other systems within the model. The macrosystem influences how individuals interact with their immediate environments and relationships, shaping their experiences and opportunities based on the societal context they inhabit. Examples include national policies on education, cultural attitudes towards gender roles, and societal norms regarding family and work.
- Exosystem: the environmental settings that indirectly influence an individual's development, even though the individual is not an active participant in these settings. The exosystem includes external factors such as a parent's workplace, community structures, and local government policies, which can impact the individual's immediate environment. These external influences shape the experiences and opportunities available to individuals through their effects on the more immediate systems around them.

- Microsystem: the innermost level of the environment that directly interacts with the individual. It includes the immediate surroundings and relationships that the person experiences daily, such as family, school, peers, and neighbourhood. The microsystem is characterized by bidirectional influences, meaning that the individual both influences and is influenced by these environments. For example, a child's development is shaped by interactions with parents, teachers, and friends, and simultaneously, the child's behaviour and characteristics affect how these relationships function. The quality and context of these interactions are crucial for the individual's development.
- Mesosystem: the interconnections between the various microsystems in an individual's life are referred to as the mesosystem. It encompasses the interactions and relationships between different settings that a person is directly involved in, such as the relationship between a child's home and school, or between their family and peer group. These interrelationships can significantly influence development by providing consistent or conflicting values, support systems, and expectations across different environments. For example, a supportive interaction between a child's parents and teachers can enhance the child's educational experience, whereas conflicting values between home and school may create stress and hinder development.

In the online safety ecosystem, we can adapt the model, readily applying the system definitions, as illustrated in Fig. 1.1.

The specific composition of stakeholders within each system may vary depending on the child and geography, but they can be broadly defined as follows:

- Microsystem: Family includes parents, siblings, and extended family, peers and neighbourhood, such as friends, fellow school pupils, and youth groups, and school and education settings, comprising teachers, support staff, school leaders and the wider school community.
- Exosystem: Encompasses the broader children's workforce with safeguarding roles, such as police, social workers, statutory bodies, and healthcare professionals, who generally will only become involved in serious online harm incidents.
- Macrosystem: Mass Media, Industry, Policy Makers, Regulators, NGOs, Academia: Stakeholders involved in national and international policy formation around online safety, which should influence

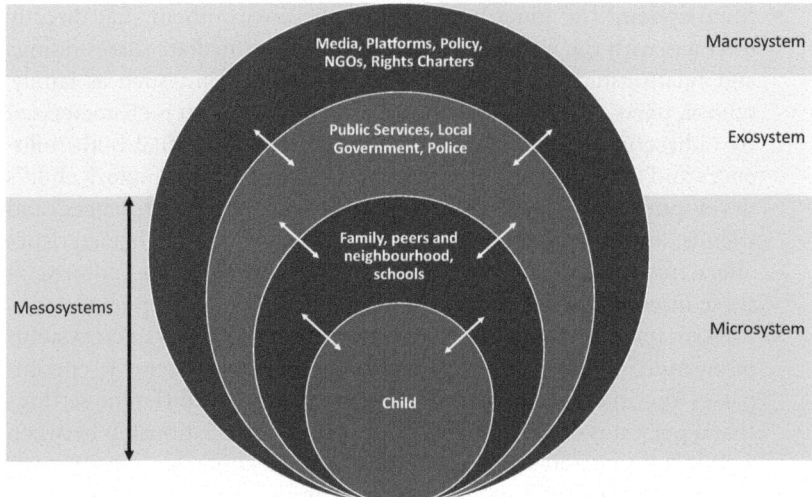

Fig. 1.1   The online safety ecosystem

the microsystems. Although these stakeholders have diverse motivations, they, hopefully, have a common goal in their commitment to child safety and achieving the best outcomes. The macrosystem will also be influenced by rights charters such as the UN Convention on the Rights of the Child, the European Convention on Human Rights, and the Universal Declaration of Human Rights.

The value of this model lies in highlighting the various stakeholders in online safeguarding and the importance of interactions (mesosystems) between those in the microsystem, as well the importance of communication between systems and the relative proximity of each stakeholder to the child. As Bronfenbrenner states, the quality of these interactions is crucial to positive outcomes for the child.

In a healthy ecosystem all stakeholders will align with the same goal—providing help and support for young people to have positive experiences online—and work together to achieve that. This means those in the macrosystem developing policy and law that is mindful of the best interests of the child and cognizant of their needs, regulators transform legislation into something enforceable and work with the stakeholders targeted by the legislation to ensure good practice, platforms develop services that consider the needs of young people, and provide tools to recognize abuse and provide tools to allow young people to disclose concerns and get effective feedback on this, NGOs and civil society play a role in advocacy to represent the authentic youth voice and provide resources and educational support for stakeholders.

In the exosystem social care, police and others with whom a young person might meet *should* be all trained to understand risk online and how to support young people with their *best interests in mind and understand that application of the law to support them in a child-centric manner.* These stakeholders should also provide clear routes for disclosure and be transparent in what will happen when disclosure occurs.

And those in the microsystem closest to the child, such as parents, wider family and schools, provide the day-to-day care and support to help them learn about online risk as they engage with more online services as they get older, and also provide an environment where young people can ask questions and be listened to, and have those questions answered without fear of punishment, unless punitive measures are appropriate to the situation.

And across all of the systems clear communication inside and across the layers should help ensure that everyone understands their role and the broader online safety ecosystem.

Adopting a holistic view of collaboration among stakeholders to support young people in online risk-taking and decision-making is more effective, as each stakeholder can contribute their expertise to the safeguarding role.

From our perspective, developed through consultation with young people and safeguarding professionals, it is crucial to shift from attempting to prevent harms to understanding that awareness of risks and reducing the risk of harm are more effective and sustainable throughout a child's lifespan.

We are not alone in this approach. Other scholars, such as Ringrose et al. (2012) and Setty (2019, 2020), align their work with a strong qualitative focus on victim representation and advocate for multi-stakeholder approaches to supporting victims. However, as we will explore below, approaches emphasizing victim support, education, and multi-stakeholder responsibility are often dismissed as too complex or burdensome and the ideal ecosystem, as described above, can be found seriously lacking.

A Note on Best Interests and the Convention on the Rights of the Child

The "best interests of the child" is a widely recognized standard in both law and child welfare practice, but its application and understanding can vary significantly. This principle seeks to ensure that decisions affecting a child—such as in custody cases, adoption, education, and healthcare—are made with the child's overall well-being as the primary concern and is enshrined in the UN Convention on the Rights of the Child. The United Nations Convention on the Rights of the Child (UNCRC) (Unicef, n.d.) is an international treaty adopted by the UN General Assembly on November 20, 1989. It was the first legally binding international instrument that recognizes and aimed to protect the full range of human rights of children, including civil, cultural, economic, political, and social rights. It has been ratified by 196 countries, making it one of the most widely ratified human rights treaties globally, except for the United States, which has signed but not ratified it.

The UNCRC is often used in explorations of online safety policy and children's rights (e.g. Bond, 2014; Livingstone & O'Neill 2014; O'Neill 2022; Livingstone et al., 2024). Indeed, the UNCRC underpinned a lot of the discussions in the first volume of this book series (Phippen, 2017) and in other work with which I have been involved (Phippen & Bond, 2023). More recently, UNICEF have updated the CRC to consider the rights of the child in digital environments under General Comment 25 (United Nations Committee on the Rights of the Child, 2021) which reiterates the importance of governments, industry, civil society and those around the child to work together for their best interests in navigating the online world.

It updates the UN Convention on the Rights of the Child (CRC) by addressing how children's rights apply within the digital world, reflecting a recognition of how deeply digital technology has permeated young lives and the resulting effects on their rights. This comment reaffirms and extends the CRC's protections, advocating for children's rights to privacy, safety, and participation within the digital realm, and it talks about the responsibilities of both governments and technology companies to actively uphold these rights.

The comment places particular emphasis on children's right to privacy in online spaces, asserting that they deserve control over their personal information. It calls for rigorous data protection standards that not only limit data collection from children but also respect their evolving ability to give informed consent as they grow. This guidance underscores that children's online safety includes protection from harmful content and exploitation; General Comment No. 25 advises that both governments and companies strengthen safeguards against cyberbullying, online abuse, and manipulative advertising.

Recognizing that the digital environment offers both opportunities and risks, the comment also stresses the need for digital literacy education. Children should have the skills to navigate online spaces responsibly and critically, and access to these educational resources should be equitable, regardless of a child's background. This aligns with another key principle—the right to freedom of expression and access to information—which is seen as particularly vital in the digital age. The digital world, the comment notes, gives children unprecedented ways to express themselves and engage with information, and states should enable children to do so safely.

However, one might argue that if the UNCRC (and General Comment 25) were widely understood in a holistic manner, and adopted into practice, given UNCRC's ratification date in many countries, surely, we should be seeing better, child-centric, practice by now? Instead, I would argue given observations that will be drawn upon throughout this book, it is often used in debate, but rarely in practice. And in debate it is often not used with a depth of understanding needed to apply it effectively.

I hear a lot from practitioners about best interests. Yet I do not see much in practice that reflects it (and this will be explored throughout this book). What is most important to grasp is that best interests should always be applied to a specific young person at a specific time, and all rights should be applied equally. However, understanding and consistently applying this standard can be challenging for several reasons. Firstly, what is considered the "best interests" can vary across cultures, individuals, and even within legal frameworks, this complexity is compounded by children having multi-dimensional needs, encompassing physical, emotional, social, and developmental aspects. Determining which needs are prioritized in specific scenarios can be contentious, especially if parents, guardians, or authorities have differing views on the child's needs (as we will discuss throughout this book). As I have already flagged as one of the most problematic narratives around online safety, while there is an increasing recognition of the importance of incorporating children's views, especially as they grow older, but this is not universally practiced and there are many examples of adults claiming that best interests, or specific rights of the child, cannot be applied (see discussion later in this book, particularly Chap. 6).

Best interests, and the rights framework in general, are continually poorly understood among practitioners, but frequently used term with which one stakeholder can attack another. For example, at the time of writing, the Australian government are proposing introducing legislation to back teens from using smartphones or having social media access.[1] While I am sure the attempted implementation and subsequent failure of this policy will be something I explore in other publications, it is currently in its infancy and not sufficiently well defined to comment upon here in detail. However, when we consider the rhetoric in the media regarding the proposed legislation, we can see ministers using the rhetoric of best interests, such as this from Australian Communications Minister Michelle Rowland:[2]

> Knowing how many children are on their sites was only one part of these important changes. I also made clear Australia's expectations that platforms must ensure the best interests of the child is at the heart of their services. This means platforms must be thinking about our children when they are making decisions about the services they offer—not just after harm occurs.

Certainly, the UN CRC is an excellent framework with which companies should be mindful when implementing online services. But given the young person and situational context in the application of best interests (Eekelaar, 1994; Freeman & Alen, 2007), it is difficult to see how ALL young people's best interests can be incorporated into global platforms. It is also becoming an increasingly used rhetorical device by NGOs, as evidenced by the Molly Rose Foundation:[3]

> If we are to better understand how we can ensure that children and young people are able to use online devices in an age-appropriate way, and in turn develop policy and regulatory responses that are in the best interests of the

---

[1] https://www.premier.sa.gov.au/media-releases/news-items/banning-social-media-for-children [Accessed October 2024]

[2] https://www.mi-3.com.au/10-09-2024/albanese-government-enact-social-media-age-limits-legislation-penciled-late-2024 [Accessed October 2024]

[3] https://mollyrosefoundation.org/june-2024party-leaders-must-make-online-safety-an-election-priority%EF%BF%BC/ [Accessed October 2024]

child, further independent evidence about the risks and benefits of using online devices is essential.

And the Internet Watch Foundation:[4]

Technologies are built to meet high standards of privacy-protection, data minimisation, proportionality, and transparency, these neither restrict nor undermine encryption. What they do is detect the illegal distribution of illegal content depicting child sexual abuse. What really matters is ensuring strong safeguards to establish a global standard. This is a policy decision, and should be based on the best interests of the child as enshrined in EU and international law.

While the UNCRC is useful as a tool to reflect upon reflection of the impact of the ecosystem on children's rights, the ecological systems theory approach is more appropriate for this analysis because one of the central theses in this book is that things that exist at the macro level rarely transfer into the microsystems, and it is these which are far more important for individual outcomes for young people in a given life course (and therefore their best interests). Or, perhaps more correctly, the framework *should* be useful if stakeholders applied it, but they do not. With complexities of best interests distilled into unchallenged media soundbites, it weakens its usefulness as a *lingua franca* for exploring online safety issues. The case in Chap. 6, so pivotal in the argument that the ecosystem is broken, around the failure of the ecosystem comprises a group of professionals who are all vocal about children's rights while failing to understand what this means or apply it.

However, it is unquestionably still important to these discussions, which is why it forms part of the macrosystem in the ecological system we apply in this analysis, and it will be referred to throughout this analysis. However, of itself, it does not allow us to unpick why policy has failed and from which source do stakeholder motivations arise. It is for this reason that, while children's rights clearly form a part of these discussions, an ecological systems theory, which places the child at the centre of the analysis (Darling, 2007), is applied rather than a rights framework.

---

[4] https://www.iwf.org.uk/news-media/blogs/imco-s-draft-opinion-weakens-online-child-protection-in-the-european-union/ [Accessed October 2024]

Exploring the Ecosystem

Therefore, in considering this analysis, and trying to understand the gulf between policy and practice, the structure of the book will move from macrosystem to those systems closer to the child and show the disconnect between different stakeholders.

The first chapter builds on previous discussions about online safety policy, focusing on the lead up to the assent of the UK Online Safety Act 2023 2023. It examines the political rhetoric and ideological motivations behind the legislation and positions it within a global context by drawing parallels with similar initiatives in Australia and the EU. The Act's evolution traces back to earlier efforts like the Digital Economy Act 2017 and marks a shift towards "platform liability", driven by political pressure and public concern about child safety online. This shift led to calls for robust age verification and stringent content moderation. The chapter critically examines the debates and consultations that shaped the Act, addressing challenges such as balancing safety with freedom of expression and privacy, and the operational and financial burdens on platforms. The role of Ofcom as the regulatory body and the penalties for non-compliance are discussed. It also explores the Digital Economy Act 2017's attempt at age verification, its subsequent challenges, and the political and media responses to its withdrawal in 2019, as well as the Online Harms White Paper and the rhetoric around creating the "safest place in the world to go online", highlighting the lack of clear definitions and the focus on industry responsibility. The concept of "duty of care" is scrutinized for its implications and potential legal complexities, while critiquing the lack of youth involvement in policy discussions, the reliance on prohibition over harm reduction, and the pervasive blame placed on "Big Tech" and algorithms. The chapter underscores the ideological persistence of regulating tech platforms through concepts like path dependence and isomorphism, which explain the tendency to follow established policy paths and adopt similar approaches across different jurisdictions. Finally, it introduces the Online Safety Act 2023, detailing its provisions, including duty of care, content moderation, transparency, age verification, and enforcement by Ofcom, while discussing the Act's operational and financial challenges and the ongoing tension between safety and freedom of expression.

Chapter 3 examines the influential role that media and professional responses play in shaping public perceptions of online harms, focusing on two recent moral panics: the Momo suicide game and COVID-19 online grooming fears. The chapter highlights how bias and opinion can over-shadow evidence-based approaches, often leading to unnecessary fear and actions among parents and educators. It critiques the sensationalist media coverage and unsupported claims that drive these panics, drawing parallels with historical events like the 1980s and 1990s Satanic Panic and argues that media narrative has more of an influence over policy direction than evidence. The chapter advocates for an evidence-based approach to dealing with online harms, stressing the importance of critical media consumption and rigorous standards in both policy and media responses. By focusing on data and evidence, the chapter argues, we can better protect young people and create a safer online environment. This chapter concludes the exploration of online safety policy, illustrating how misinformed stakeholders and moral panics do little to help young people, ultimately scapegoating industry while ignoring the roles of other stakeholders.

Chapter 4 begins a detailed exploration of the exo- and microsystems drawing upon large datasets to argue that what happens closer to the child has little relationship with what is discussed in the macrosystems. It explores the translation of national online safety policies into school practices through the analysis data from the 360 Degree Safe and ProjectEVOLVE platforms and reveals how schools implement statutory responsibilities regarding online safety. The findings highlight significant gaps in areas requiring long-term resource investment and broader stakeholder engagement, such as staff training and governor awareness, despite well-established policies and technical measures. ProjectEVOLVE data shows a stark contrast in the use of online safety resources, with primary schools extensively using them while secondary schools underutilize them. The focus tends to be on less complex topics like online relationships and self-image over more technical aspects like privacy and security. This suggests a need for more balanced digital literacy education across all educational stages. Overall, the chapter indicates that while national policies provide clear guidance, their implementation in schools is inconsistent, often falling short of intended outcomes, revealing a disconnect between policy and practice that starts to highlight fissures in the ecosystem.

Chapter 5 of the book, titled "The Silent Youth Voice", delves into the significant gap between grassroots evidence and policy directions concerning online harms, emphasizing the often-overlooked perspectives of young people. Despite claims by many policy makers to represent youth voices, the chapter reveals that authentic concerns of young people—such as peer conflict, social media anxiety, and the impact of current affairs—are frequently ignored in favour of focusing on edge cases and extreme content like pornography and terrorism to inform policy developments. Through a survey of over 16,000 young people, the chapter highlights several key findings: young people are more likely to seek help from peers than uninformed adults; they distrust platform-based reporting tools; and they are frustrated with the poorly informed, punitive support from adults, including teachers and parents. The chapter concludes by pointing out the persistent disconnect between youth voices and policy actions, urging for better engagement and support from adult stakeholders.

Chapter 6 is arguably the pivotal chapter of the book, in that it contends that this platform-centric focus fails to address the crucial role of other stakeholders, such as educators and informed adults, in supporting young people. The chapter advocates for a balanced approach combining regulation, education, and stakeholder collaboration to create a safer digital environment and presents a case study pivotal as a demonstration of how platform liability can never resolve the issues young people face online without the involvement of other stakeholders closer to the child who need to realize their responsibilities lie beyond being punitive figures. An essential case study, it demonstrates the impact of poor practice in the micro- and exosystem to show how let down young people can be by adults purported to have their best interests in mind, and how easily adults with responsibility for safeguarding can fall back on victim blaming and poor subject knowledge when supposedly supporting a young person. Furthermore, it shows how disconnected the ecosystem has become and argues that, in its present form, it is broken and will continue to fail young people, even though stakeholders within it all claim that the goal is to keep them safe from harm. And in drawing these discussions to a close, it argues that the ecosystem model allows us to observe the safeguarding dystopia in a far more holistic manner.

In conclusion, this book highlights the critical need for a paradigm shift in online safety policy towards a more holistic, multi-stakeholder approach that genuinely incorporates the voices and needs of young people. Despite significant legislative efforts like the UK's Online Safety Act 2023, current policies remain overly reliant on simplistic prohibitions and technological interventions, failing to address the complexities of online harm effectively. The analysis calls for an evidence-based strategy focused on education, empowerment, and harm reduction, moving away from punitive measures. Only by engaging families, schools, public services, and the tech industry in a coordinated effort can we hope to create a safer, more supportive digital environment for young people. The future of online safety depends on recognizing the diverse experiences of young users and fostering an inclusive, proactive approach that empowers them to navigate the digital world responsibly.

REFERENCES

Bond, E. (2014). *Childhood, mobile technologies and everyday experiences.* Palgrave.

Bronfenbrenner, U. (1979). *The ecology of human development: Experiments by nature and design.* Harvard University Press.

Darling, N. (2007). Ecological systems theory: The person in the center of the circles. *Research in Human Development, 4*(3–4), 203–217.

Eekelaar, J. (1994). The interests of the child and the child's wishes: The role of dynamic self-determinism. *International Journal of Law, Policy and the Family, 8*(1), 42–61.

Freeman, M. D., & Alen, A. (2007). *Article 3: The best interests of the child* (Vol. 3). Martinus Nijhoff.

Lacohée, H., Phippen, A. D., & Furnell, S. M. (2006). Risk and restitution: Assessing how users establish online trust. *Computers & Security, 25*(7), 486–493.

Livingstone, S., & O'Neill, B. (2014). Children's rights online: Challenges, dilemmas and emerging directions. In S. van der Hof, B. van den Berg, & B. Schermer (Eds.), *Minding minors wandering the web: Regulating online child safety* (Information technology and law series) (Vol. 24, pp. 19–38). Springer with T. M. C. Asser Press.

Livingstone, S., Third, A., & Lansdown, G. (2024). Children vs adults: Negotiating UNCRC General comment No. 25 on childrens rights in the digital environment. In *Handbook of media and communication governance* (pp. 414–428). Edward Elgar Publishing.

O'Neill, B. (2022). Online safety and empowerment in a global context. In D. Lemish (Ed.), *The Routledge international handbook of children, adolescents, and media.* Routledge International.

Phippen, A. (2017). *Children's online behaviour and safety: Policy and rights challenges.* Springer.

Phippen, A., & Bond, E. (2022). *Online safeguarding vulnerable adults: Multi-agency perspectives on rights to participation and protection online.* Policy Press.

Phippen, A., & Bond, E. (2023). *Policing teen sexting—Supporting children's rights while applying the law.* Palgrave Macmillan.

Ringrose, J., Gill, R., Livingstone, S., & Harvey, L. (2012). *A qualitative study of children, young people and 'sexting': A report prepared for the NSPCC.*

Setty, E. (2019). A rights-based approach to youth sexting: Challenging risk, shame, and the denial of rights to bodily and sexual expression within youth digital sexual culture. *International Journal of Bullying Prevention, 1*(4), 298–311.

Setty, E. (2020). *Risk and harm in youth sexting: Young people's perspectives.* Routledge.

Unicef. (n.d.). *UNCRC convention on the rights of the child.* Accessed October 2024, from https://www.unicef.org.uk/what-we-do/un-convention-child-rights/

United Nations Committee on the Rights of the Child. (2021). *General Comment No. 25 (2021) on children's rights in relation to the digital environment. CRC/C/GC/25, 2021.* Accessed October 2024, from https://tbinternet.ohchr.org/Treaties/CRC/Shared%20Documents/1_Global/CRC_C_GC_25_8785_E.pdf

CHAPTER 2

The Rhetoric of Online Safety and the Five-Year Policy Cycle

Abstract This chapter analyses the political and ideological factors shaping the UK's Online Safety Act 2023, presenting it as a case study of the rhetorical and legislative landscape around child online safety. Tracing the act's development from early policy discussions, the chapter critiques a "duty of care" model that centres on platform liability, emphasizing an ideological stance that seeks to control tech industry practices. The chapter examines the growing trend of "platform scapegoating", where complex societal issues like child safety are attributed largely to digital platforms, sidelining other influential factors. By contextualizing the Act within broader international policies such as Australia's Online Safety Act 2023 and the EU's Digital Services Act, the text explores the global convergence towards a regulatory stance prioritizing punitive measures over multi-stakeholder involvement. Through an analysis of the path-dependent and isomorphic tendencies in policy making, this chapter reveals how the UK's legislative approach to online safety, driven by political rhetoric and platform liability, overlooks the nuanced needs of young people and effective harm reduction strategies.

Keywords Online Safety Act 2023 • Platform liability • Duty of care • Policy rhetoric • Child digital protection

A. Phippen, *Policy and Rights Challenges in Children's Online Behaviour and Safety, 2017–2023*,
https://doi.org/10.1007/978-3-031-80286-7_2

A primary journey explored in this text is the UK's Online Safety Act 2023, which reached royal assent at the end of 2023 and is met with the frequent successor statement "Making the UK the safest place to go online in the world" (UK Government, 2017a). This legislation, whose origins can be seen to develop since David Cameron's 2012 speech on online safety (Phippen, 2017), and the culmination of considerable debate, media coverage, and stakeholder demands, shows, arguably, what happens when adultist agendas take to the fore against claims of "saving" children from the perils of the internet. While this piece of legislation is the primary vehicle to deconstruct policy, rhetoric and juxtapose with evidence, there are several international parallels (such as Australia's Online Safety Act 2023 (Australian Government, 2021) and EU's Digital Services Act (European Union, 2022)). The Australian legislation, which made it onto the statute books before the UK version (in January 2022), adopts a similar "duty of care" model so is a useful comparator of impact. At the time of writing while there has been a lot of noise around the act, there remain few actions carried out. However, this does give us a window into what might be to come of the UK Online Safety Act 2023 (UK Government, 2023). This chapter will explore the route to the online safety act, prior to the subsequent chapter trying to understand why the macrosystems exist in their current state.

Furthermore, while the legislative development will be a policy focus for this book, giving it has taken central stage in UK policy, it is used predominantly as a means to explore discourse and narratives around online harms, rather than being a detail exploration of the legislation itself (which will feature in a subsequent book once the regulatory powers associated with the legislation are finally in place and we have a means of assessing its impact). In doing so, we explore a central question in both the previous volume of this book and in this one—why do the policy approaches used fail to address the youth voice and develop approaches that do little to address what they ask for?

This chapter picks up where the first volume finished. The previous monograph considered online safety policy at a time where there was growing political interest in preventing access to "harmful" content, and stamping out upsetting online behaviour using digital technology, and political pressure on service providers, to achieve this. While this direction ultimately resulted in the Online Safety Act 2023 2023 (ibid.), this is something that has arisen from detailed policy discussions (engaged a lot of the time in the media) that first arose (discussed previously over ten years ago in 2012). In this chapter we explore the build up to the Online Safety Act 2023 as a case study in political rhetoric around child online safety, and what became an ideological obsession by a government to not leave regulation to "tech billionaires".[1] The UK Online Safety Act 2023 2023 is claimed to be a landmark piece of legislation aimed at enhancing digital safety and regulating online content, particularly to protect children from harmful and illegal material. This chapter delves into the complex journey leading up to the Act's implementation, highlighting the political rhetoric and ideological motivations that shaped its development.

Through a detailed exploration of the legislative process, the chapter underscores how the Act evolved as a response to mounting political pressure to safeguard children online. It traces the origins of the Act back to earlier legislative efforts, such as the Digital Economy Act 2017 (UK Government, 2017b), and examines the ideological shift towards imposing greater responsibility on tech platforms—a concept known as "platform liability" (Woods & Perrin, 2021) The narrative reveals the persistent political discourse advocating for robust age verification measures and stringent content moderation to prevent access to harmful content.

The chapter critically examines the debates and consultations that shaped the Online Safety Act 2023, highlighting the challenges of balancing safety with freedom of expression and privacy. It also addresses the practical implications of implementing the Act, noting the significant operational and financial burdens placed on online platforms. Furthermore, it discusses the role of the Office of Communications (Ofcom) as the regulatory body tasked with enforcing compliance and the potential penalties for non-compliant companies.

Now, Where Were We?

The first book concluded with an introduction to the concept of the *Safeguarding Dystopia*—where children's rights were eroded in order to keep them safe, and suggested that a change of direction is needed if we are to actually support and empower young people in this area.

This book will begin by reviewing this analysis and propose that, rather than adopt more progressive, rights-based approaches, the current policy landscape seems to have become even more narrow, particularly with the

---

[1] https://hansard.parliament.uk/Commons/2021-11-18/debates/13A7EB7D-9C4C-40BE-84E4-7230578DF9B3/HarmfulContentOnline [Accessed October 2024]

introduction of the Online Safety Bill and its focus entirely on platform liability and duty of care. One of my frustrations in this field is the lack of learning from history by those who make policy. Perhaps an excellent example of this is the reflect upon what was, arguably, the policy staring point in the UK for online safety, and where we currently are with the recently assented Online Safety Act 2023 2023 (ibid.) and subsequent policy discussions.

The Byron Review, officially titled "Safer Children in a Digital World", was commissioned by the UK government in 2007 to address increasing concerns about the digital safety of children (Byron Review, 2008). As internet usage among children soared, the review aimed to tackle issues related to their exposure to harmful or inappropriate online content, cyberbullying, and the impact of violent video games. This surge in digital engagement, it was proposed, highlighted the need for comprehensive strategies to protect young users and provide parents with the necessary tools and knowledge to guide their children's online experiences. The review sought to speak to a wide range of stakeholders, evaluate existing measures, identify gaps, and recommend improvements to ensure a safer digital environment for children.

A significant motivation behind the Byron Review was the recognition of a generational digital divide, where many parents lacked sufficient understanding of digital technologies, leading to a need for better resources and educational initiatives. *The review emphasized the importance of a collective approach involving government, industry, and families to foster a safer digital world for children.* The emphasis here is deliberate, and something we will return to many times when reflecting on where we are now.

The review made several key recommendations:

- Establishing a UK Council for Child Internet Safety (UKCCIS): To bring together various stakeholders, including government, industry, and charities, to implement and oversee strategies to improve children's online safety.
- Better Education and Awareness: Recommending educational programmes for children, parents, and teachers to promote digital literacy and safe online behaviour.
- Clearer Age Ratings for Video Games: Simplifying the age rating system for video games and ensuring better enforcement of these ratings to prevent children from accessing inappropriate content.

- Improving Parental Controls: Encouraging the development and use of parental control software and settings to help parents monitor and manage their children's online activities. [Some success, but not well used as they tended to not be very effective.]
- Research and Evidence: Conducting ongoing research to understand the impact of the digital world on children and to ensure that policies are based on robust evidence.
- Industry Standards and Best Practices: Working with the industry to develop standards and best practices for protecting children online, including content moderation and safer social networking services.
- Reporting and Regulation: Improving mechanisms for reporting harmful or inappropriate online content and ensuring effective regulatory oversight.

These recommendations aimed, it was proposed, to create a safer online environment for children, promote responsible digital citizenship, and ensure that parents and educators are better equipped to support children's use of digital technologies. The government of the time promised to implement the recommendations, and many stakeholders heralded the holistic, multi-stakeholder approach it adopted as the progressive way forward.

We fast forward now to May 2024, where in the UK parliament there was a debate entitled "Smartphones and Social Media: Children" motivated by an ePetition calling for a ban on smartphones and social media for children under 16.[2]

In the debate, Miriam Cates, the then MP for Penistone and Stocksbridge, who had a track record of prohibitionist approaches to tackline online issues (Cates, 2024) initiated a debate on the impact of smartphones and social media on children. She painted a stark picture, likening the digital world to a lawless land where children are exposed to extreme violence, bullying, and sexual harassment daily. She highlighted the alarming rise in suicide rates, self-harm, and anxiety among children since the advent of smartphones and social media and referenced Professor Jonathan Haidt's recently published book (Haidt, 2024), which has already become

---

[2] https://hansard.parliament.uk/Commons/2024-05-14/debates/9EEEE3FC-7B2A-45E4-87E8-9449B603B1D9/SmartphonesAndSocialMediaChildren [Accessed October 2024]

the subject of much challenge,[3] which points to a link between these trends and the proliferation of smartphones and social media since 2010, with a notable surge from 2014 onwards.

The discussion emphasized the gender-specific effects of social media. For girls, it was claimed, platforms like Instagram, TikTok, and Snapchat amplify pressures of visual social comparison, leading to body image issues, increased cases of gender confusion, and sexual harassment. Boys, on the other hand, suffer from the isolating effects of gaming and pornography, which distort their perceptions of relationships and sex.

Parents, too, it was argued, are under immense pressure to allow their children to have smartphones, fearing social isolation for their children if they don't comply. This peer pressure complicates efforts to control children's screen time and online activities.

In schools, smartphone use is a significant distraction, negatively impacting students' academic performance. Schools that enforce effective phone bans tend to perform better academically, with higher grades and better Ofsted ratings. The debate called attention to the need for robust online safety measures and the Online Safety Act 2023 2023 was recognized as a step forward, holding technology companies accountable for children's safety online. However, MPs argued that *more* regulation is needed, including effective age verification to prevent children from accessing harmful content.

Within the debate, most stakeholders were positioned as victims of harm and being unable to cope. However, one stakeholder, the platforms who provided these services, and the industry who sell mobile devices, should be doing more to stop these harms from occurring.

Several solutions were proposed during the debate. These included enforcing phone bans in schools, raising the legal age for social media use to 16, and improving age verification mechanisms. There were calls for funding to provide phone pouches or lockers in schools to ensure phones are not accessible during school hours. The idea of developing child-safe phones, which lack internet access, was also floated to protect younger children from exposure to harmful content. Finally, and in contrast with all other proposals, a public health campaign to educate parents about the risks associated with smartphone and internet use for young children was suggested. But we should note the suggestion was not to develop parental

---

[3] https://blogs.lse.ac.uk/parenting4digitalfuture/2024/05/15/haidt/   [Accessed October 2024]

responsibility, just to tell them that allowing their children to use devices and social media was harmful.

MPs shared personal anecdotes and highlighted the dangers posed by smartphones and social media. They emphasized the need for collective action and government intervention to protect children. There were also calls for increased research into the physical and mental impacts of screen use on children, and a recognition that while parents play a crucial role, broader societal and regulatory measures are essential.

The debate underscored the urgent need for comprehensive measures to address the harmful effects of smartphones and social media on children. MPs from across the political spectrum expressed strong support for tougher regulations and interventions to safeguard children's mental and physical well-being.

The debate concluded with this statement from Ms Cates, delivered unironically:

> I want to make a final point: this is not a debate about liberty, freedom, parenting or technology; it is a debate about child development. The human brain is not wired to learn from passive consumption; it is wired to learn from real-life interaction. That is how children learn. However safe we make the internet from damaging content, children will never gain the skills, knowledge and wellbeing they need from staring at a screen. They will always need real-life interaction. That is why we must restrict screens and ban social media for under-16s —because otherwise they will never learn.

While such approaches might gain media attention and show a public mask of holding platforms to account, does it have any chance of achieving the claimed goal of keeping citizens, and particularly children, safe online?

In the previous volume (Phippen, 2017), we explored the early stages post Byron of the move from the multi-stakeholder, child-centric approach called for in that review (and potentially dismissed due to a change of government in 2010) to the *safeguarding dystopia* that assumed that, in order to keep children safe, technological interventions that prevented harm can be implemented. In 2024, when politicians are debating removing children's access to smartphones, I might suggest that, if anything, the policy space has become more dystopian and prohibitive.

So how did we end up here?

The First Death of Age Verification (2017)

In April 2017 the Digital Economy Act (UK Government, 2017b) achieved royal assent and the UK Government stated its intentions[4] to "be a world leader in the digital economy". Within this legislation, specifically Part 3, there was a focus on what the government referred to as "protections for children online". They claimed the act would:[5]

- introduce age verification checks for access to all websites and "apps" containing pornographic material
- protect children from content that is not suitable for them, and can potentially harm them
- ensure that our offline laws and protections are also applicable online, as children increasingly live their lives online

And in order to achieve this they would:

- introduce a new requirement in law for commercial providers to establish robust age verification controls for online pornographic content in the UK
- establish a new regulatory framework backed by civil sanctions to monitor, notify, and enforce compliance with the law
- work with payments providers (Visa, Mastercard, PayPal, and others) and ancillary services to enable them to withdraw their services from infringing sites

Clearly highlighting an ideological position that technology must be the solution to these issues because any content which might be considered harmful is accessed online. The Act made it clear that any commercial pornography provider allowing access to their services from the UK must provide age verification to ensure only people over the age of 18 are able to consume pornographic content. Note that the term *commercial* did not necessarily relate to pay for access services. A site making income from

---

[4] https://www.gov.uk/government/collections/digital-economy-bill-2016   [Accessed October 2024]

[5] https://assets.publishing.service.gov.uk/government/uploads/system/uploads/attachment_data/file/535010/6._Age_Verification_Fact_Sheet.pdf   [Accessed October 2024]

advertising but providing pornography for free would be equally account-able as a result of making money through advertising revenue.

A persistent political message since 2012 was "We should stop young people from accessing pornography" and a lot of the safeguarding dysto-pia concept in the previous text explored tools that tried, and failed to do this, while also, potentially, impact their rights.

What has evolved from this political direction is the re-emergence of what can be referred to as "platform liability"—the belief that platforms have a liability for the content, and access to that content, on their plat-forms and therefore the key stakeholder to be able to address these issues. The concept of platform liability has existed from the early years of online technology but has evolved significantly, particularly as digital platforms have become central to economic and social activities. This evolution can be broadly categorized in a number of stages.

During the early years of the internet, or more correctly, the World Wide Web, in the early 1990s, platform liability was largely uncharted ter-ritory. The focus of law at the time was more on encouraging growth and innovation (Citron & Wittes, 2018). However, a pivotal moment came in the US with the passage of the Communications Decency Act (CDA) in 1996, particularly Section 230 (Ehrlich, 2002), which provided broad immunity to online platforms from liability for third-party content. Specifically, Section 230(c)(1) of the act states:

> Section 230(c)(1) - Treatment of publisher or speaker
> No provider or user of an interactive computer service shall be treated as the publisher or speaker of any information provided by another informa-tion content provider.

This provision provides immunity to online platforms and users from being held liable for content created by third parties. This was seen as essential for the growth and freedom of the internet and has since become the centre of considerable debate around whether this should still stand (Goldman, 2017).

More recently, as we will explore below, platform liability, in tandem with the complimentary concept of "Duty of Care", is very much the favoured approach of policy makers in the regulation of technology plat-forms from the perspective of online child safety (and also, to a lesser degree, the safety of all users on platforms). The debate around platform liability has become more nuanced, focusing on the balance between protecting user speech and controlling harmful content (Gillespie, 2017). In the US, discussions about amending or repealing Section 230 have become more frequent, with arguments that the law enables platforms to shirk responsibility for harmful content (ibid.). Similarly, other countries began implementing or considering stricter regulations for digital platforms to hold them more accountable for content, such as the UK's Online Safety Bill, which is the focus in this chapter. However, different countries have taken various approaches to platform liability, for instance, countries like China and Russia exert more control and demand higher compliance from platforms concerning government directives (Flonk, 2021).

Returning to the Digital Economy Act, arguably, this was the first time in the UK platform liability around access to harmful content was put into law.

However, once the bill had achieved royal assent, it became apparent that there were some technical challenges in how one might implement the age verification measures demanded in the legislation. One of the interesting questions lay in what constitutes a pornography provider—given there is much pornography on much more broad social media platforms and could be shared by end users in peer networks. A statutory instrument was published to clarify this—the Online Pornography (Commercial Basis) Regulations 2019 (UK Government, 2019a). In this instrument, it is stated that a site would not be subject to age verification if less than *one-third* of its content is pornographic. Again, a somewhat arbitrary measure which would be difficult to quantify (or apply in the courts if one was to argue a platform had failed in its liabilities)—for example, does this relate to file capacity (i.e. the amount of pornographic content in megabytes/total site content in megabytes), file count (i.e. given the number of files on the site, are over one-third pornographic) or whether this relates to overall content (e.g. administration and other publicly inaccessible files), or only files that could potentially be served to an end user. This was a very simple illustration about how stating something technical within law can result in unintended consequences for those tasked with implementing the legislation.

Subsequently, the British Board of Film Classification (BBFC) was appointed as the Age Verification regulator, responsible for the enforcement section of the Digital Economy Act legislation. It was granted powers that were intended to come into force by the end of 2018, then April 2019, then July 2019, to enforce the legislation including the means to request social media companies and search engines to remove services (to address the fact that while social media companies were not "one-third" pornography and therefore not liable for age verification, they could be rich sources of pornographic content), request withdrawal of service from payment providers, and instructing Internet Service Providers to block non-compliant sites.

For some (myself included), the announcement on October 16, 2019, in a written statement, the Secretary of State for Digital, Culture, Media and Sport, Nicky Morgan, that Part 3 of the Digital Economy Act 2017 would not be commenced[6] came as no surprise. It was the view of the government that the regulatory framework detailed in the emerging Online Harms White Paper (UK Government, 2019b) (see below) would be a more consistent approach to tackling the harms related to young people's access to pornography (as ever, without defining what an online harm might be).

The Digital Economy Act objectives will, therefore, be delivered through our proposed online harms regulatory regime. This course of action will give the regulator discretion on the most effective means for companies to meet their duty of care. As currently drafted, the Digital Economy Act does not cover social media platforms.

> We are committed to the UK becoming a world-leader in the development of online safety technology and to ensure companies of all sizes have access to, and adopt, innovative solutions to improve the safety of their users. This includes age verification tools and we expect them to continue to play a key role in protecting children online.

Unsurprisingly, the more hysterical parts of social media and blogging ramped up the rhetoric and highlighted exactly why this issue requires informed, calm debate. It was suggested by "one of the world's leading authorities on children's and young people's use of digital technologies" on their blog[7] that the withdrawal of the age verification:

> condemned Britain's children to being exposed to horrific scenes of sexual violence for a further two, three, maybe four or more years.

---

[6] https://www.parliament.uk/business/publications/written-questions-answers-statements/written-statement/Commons/2019-10-16/HCWS13/ [Accessed October 2024]
[7] https://johncarr.blog/2019/10/16/with-steam-coming-out-of-my-ears/ [Accessed October 2024]

This comment was echoed in the House of Lords,[8] where similar rhetoric was used:

> We are talking about violent sexual content, gang rape, real and close-up images of sexual acts, all just one click away because there are no age restrictions. (Baroness Benjamin)

Again, I should stress that scenes of sexual violence are clearly defined as illegal under the well-established (albeit poor enacted) "extreme pornography" legislation—Section 63 of the Criminal Justice and Immigration Act 2008 (UK Government, 2008) and is certainly not something accessible through mainstream pornography providers. To refer to all pornography as sexual violence simply stokes moral outrage and detracts from sensible, objective discussion on the subject. To reiterate—mainstream pornography is legal in the UK.

THE BIRTH OF THE ONLINE SAFETY ACT 2023

In April 2019, the UK Government released its Online Harms White Paper (ibid.) to much press coverage and ministerial comment on how it will ensure that the UK is *the safest place in the world to go online*, while supporting and growing the UK as a world leader in digital business. It aimed to set out both the problem domain and solutions that included a regulatory framework, an independent regulator for "online safety", the scope of companies within this framework, how enforcement might work, the role of technology, and the empowerment of the end user.

The white paper had its roots in the Internet Safety Strategy green paper (UK Government, 2017c) and green paper response[9] which emerged around the time the Digital Economy Act reached assent. Perhaps the first surprise for those of us who had been anticipating this document, it was no longer about Internet Safety but Online Harms. However, the white paper makes little effort to define what an "Online Harm" actually is, aside from the following from the ministerial introduction which states:

---

[8] https://hansard.parliament.uk/Lords/2019-10-22/debates/7DB58FBA-ABFE-4037-84AC-103A1555D4CD/ [Accessed October 2024]

[9] https://assets.publishing.service.gov.uk/government/uploads/system/uploads/attachment_data/file/708873/Government_Response_to_the_Internet_Safety_Strategy_Green_Paper_-_Final.pdf [Accessed October 2024]

Online harms are widespread and can have serious consequences.

In terms of presenting balance, there is neither a clear definition of online safety. Therefore, establishing a path on forming legislation to address an intangible end goal.

Both law and algorithms (which, as Lessig [2009] argues, defines the law of cyberspace) require clear definition if they are to be successfully implemented. Algorithms and code are no good at subjective interpretation, they simply follow the instructions coded within them. Vague definitions to prevent harms are not a good specification for any technical implementation.

Nevertheless, the rhetoric around "safety" and unacceptability of harmful content is set out from the outset of the paper without actually defining it:

> The government wants the UK to be the safest place in the world to go online, and the best place to start and grow a digital business. Given the prevalence of illegal and harmful content online, and the level of public concern about online harms, not just in the UK but worldwide, we believe that the digital economy urgently needs a new regulatory framework to improve our citizens' safety online.
>
> Illegal and unacceptable content and activity is widespread online, and UK users are concerned about what they see and experience on the internet. The prevalence of the most serious illegal content and activity, which threatens our national security or the physical safety of children, is unacceptable. Online platforms can be a tool for abuse and bullying, and they can be used to undermine our democratic values and debate. The impact of harmful content and activity can be particularly damaging for children, and there are growing concerns about the potential impact on their mental health and wellbeing.

It continues:

> There is currently a range of regulatory and voluntary initiatives aimed at addressing these problems, but these have not gone far or fast enough, or been consistent enough between different companies, to keep UK users safe online ....

... The UK will be the first to do this, leading international efforts by setting a coherent, proportionate and effective approach that reflects our commitment to a free, open and secure internet.

... We want technology itself to be part of the solution, and we propose measures to boost the tech-safety sector in the UK, as well as measures to help users manage their safety online.

... Tackling harmful content and activity online is one part of the UK's wider ambition to develop rules and norms for the internet, including protecting personal data, supporting competition in digital markets and promoting responsible digital design.

A focus of ethno-centric moral positions and a wish to be world leader in online safety suggests a lack of understanding about how online technology works, and one that is arguably imperialistic in tone. And again, this rhetoric informs the foundation of a legislative narrative focussed entirely on the responsibilities of a single stakeholder—industry, and a model of "duty of care" (Woods & Perrin, 2021) to achieve this.

The concept of "duty of care" for tech platforms is relatively recent and has evolved alongside the increasing influence and impact of these platforms on society. While specific legal formulations and legislative efforts have varied by jurisdiction, the broader notion of imposing a duty of care on tech platforms started gaining significant traction in the late 2010s and early 2020s (ibid.).

The idea of imposing a duty of care on tech companies began to be discussed more earnestly in policy and academic circles as social media and other tech platforms grew in influence and societal impact (Balkin, 2021). Early discussions often centred around issues like online harassment, misinformation, and the spread of harmful content. The UK Online Harms White Paper is one of the most prominent early instances of proposing a formal duty of care for tech platforms. However, the model has been adopted in other jurisdictions, such as the European Union's Digital Services Act (DSA) (ibid.) and Australia's Online Safety Act 2023 2021 (ibid.), which includes measures to increase the accountability of tech platforms and enforce a duty of care to protect users from online harm, including cyberbullying and the spread of harmful content.

Within the white paper much was made around the expectation of a "Duty of Care" for digital companies who might fall under the gaze of the new regulator:

> The government will establish a new statutory duty of care to make companies take more responsibility for the safety of their users and tackle harm caused by content or activity on their services.

However, again, there seems to be little attempt to define or delineate whether this aligns with the broader legal concept of duty of care, and its relationship with the tort of negligence. Is the duty of care in the white paper being defined as a form a negligence, and if so, how might the company be able to demonstrate due diligence or protect itself from vexatious claims of harm? Negligence is the subject of much legal debate and is certainly not getting any less complex, as rather beautifully exclaimed in Deakin and Markesinis's (2012) Tort Law:

> The experience of the last thirty years or so if anything, suggests a dialectical process of evolution with many, often inexplicable, tergiversations.

Throughout the paper the discourse on the intention to adopt a "risk-based approach" is flawed and is based on rhetoric rather than reality. The language and tone of how children and young people are referred to throughout the paper treats them as a single, passive entity. For example, the paper stated: *"Users want to be empowered to manage their online safety, and that of their children, but there is insufficient support in place and they currently feel vulnerable online"*, which completely fails to acknowledge that children are users in their own right and depicts children as "passive" consumers of internet content rather than "active" users and contributors to the digital economy.

The Online Harms White Paper also introduced the bold claim that has since become a common political trope from UK politicians:

> Many of our international partners are also developing new regulatory approaches to tackle online harms, but none has yet established a regulatory framework that tackles this range of online harms. The UK will be the first to do this, leading international efforts by setting a coherent, proportionate and effective approach that reflects our commitment to a free, open and secure internet.

COMMITTEE STAGE—SHOULD POLICY BE DRIVEN BY EVIDENCE?

Young people, I was amazed to learn, consume huge amounts of television via YouTube.

Nadine Dorries, Secretary of State for Digital, Culture, Media, and Sport.[10]

The above quote comes from a debate on BBC funding on January 17, 2022. While it might be easy to approach this quotation with derision and a mocking tone, perhaps it is better to view it as an illustration of a serious indication that while our law makers might know how in-depth knowledge on a subject does no dampen their enthusiasm to develop legislation related to it.

Another step to explore in the path to the Online Safety Act 2023 2023 was the Joint Select Committee for the Draft Online Safety Bill (UK Government, 2021), who produced a detailed report on their recommendations for the developing legislation at the end of 2021 (Joint Committee on the Draft Online Safety Bill, 2021) following a detailed inquiry, and after the Christmas recess there was a debate[11] in the House of Commons. The report was 193 pages long and comprises 127 recommendations and again there is not sufficient space to explore it in depth. However, as further data point on our exploration of political rhetoric and motivation for the Online Safety Act 2023, it is extremely useful. It draws on key aspects of online safeguarding and how the committee, and fellow parliamentarians, consider how to tackle these, against a backdrop of shallow knowledge and what could be referred to as opinion as fact. Never strong foundations for effective legislation.

The Bill by this stage was an ambitious and sizable piece of work that developed the duty of care concept further. And while there were sensible suggestions in the report for greater accuracy around what does and does not constitute harmful content (including the removal of a term in the draft bill that called for that platforms should address any content that might be harmful to adults, as adjudged by the wonderfully vague "adult of ordinary sensibilities". It also raised concerns about given too much

---

[10] https://hansard.parliament.uk/Commons/2022-01-17/debates/7E590668-43C9-4 3D8-9C49-9D29B8530977/ [Accessed October 2024]

[11] https://hansard.parliament.uk/Commons/2022-01-13/debates/1B9767E0-EF19-4D77-8C73-AADA64365D2C/DraftOnlineSafetyBillReport [Accessed October 2024]

unaccountable power to the secretary of state to modify codes of practice, and questioned the validity of senior management liability for any online harms that might arise on the platform (raising once again the question of what "doing enough" looks like) at a criminal level.

However, there was also a strong rhetoric throughout the report which might have been considered grandstanding, or perhaps motivated by showing other stakeholders how serious these issues are and how duties need to be taken seriously.

As an early reflection, while the report claimed "*Protecting children is a key objective of the draft Bill and our report*", there was not a single young person asked to give oral evidence in the committee inquiry, and while many youth charities and those who work with children and young people submitted written evidence, there is scant evidence that the people the report claims are at the heart of the new legislation were consulted at all.

This is a perennial challenge in the online safeguarding arena. Adultist agendas, "doing it for the kids", decide the best thing to do is stop bad things happening, and stop young people doing bad things, rather than engaging in discourse with them to understand their needs and requirements. This conflicts with what young people tell us, as reflected in Chap. 5.

Indeed, in the summary document[12] that was published by the committee alongside the full report, opens with the statement:

Big tech has failed its chance to self-regulate

The Online Safety Bill is the Government's chance to make the internet safer for all

The concept of Big Tech as the evil stakeholder is something that has become de rigueur in a lot of online safety policy debates at all levels of the ecosystem and was a clear sign of the emergence of what can only be referred to now as platform scapegoating. That is not to say platforms do not have a role to play in the ecosystem, they obviously do. However, others do as well, and platforms cannot be to blame for everything that happens online, no matter how politically attractive it is to claim this.

---

[12] https://ukparliament.shorthandstories.com/draft-online-safety-bill-joint-committee-report/index.html [Accessed October 2024]

The rhetoric still relies on the "Big tech" terms, as if rich billionaires are the only people who will be affected by this legislation. The term clearly positions us, the regular citizen, against these evil, exploitative corporations, responsible for some many of the harms in the world today. It fails to mention the potentially thousands of small companies and start-ups who might fall under the reach of the Bill if there are providing user-to-user or search services as part of their platform offer and the literally billions of people who freely choose to engage with these "evil" platforms on a daily basis.

The key recommendations of the report were

1. What's illegal offline should be regulated online
2. Ofcom[13] should issue binding Codes of Practice
3. New criminal offences are needed
4. Keep children safe from accessing pornography

As a starting point, this is reasonable, if taken at face value.

However, after this introduction, the document continues to make further outlandish claims which do not stand up quite so well to scrutiny:

The human cost of an unregulated internet can be counted in:

- mass murder in Myanmar
- intensive care beds full of unvaccinated covid-19 patients
- insurrection at the US Capitol
- teenagers sent down rabbit holes of content promoting self-harm, eating disorders and suicide.

Doubling down on this view, in the opening statement in the debate following publication of the report, Damien Collins, the Committee chair, stated:

The big tech companies have had plenty of notice that this is coming. During that period, have we seen a marked improvement? Have we seen the introduction of effective self-regulation? Have the companies set a challenge to Parliament, saying "You don't really need to pass this legislation, because

---

[13] The UK Telecommunications Regulator

we are doing all we can already"? No. If anything, the problems have got worse. Last year, we saw an armed insurrection in Washington DC in which a mob stormed the Capitol building, fuelled by messages of hate and confrontation that circulated substantially online. Last summer, members of the England football team were subject to vile racist abuse at the end of the final—the football authorities had warned the companies that that could happen, but they did not prepare for it or act adequately at the time.

The last sentence is particularly telling—how could platforms have pre-emptively determined who might be posting racial abuse of footballers and prevented it from being posted if those posting did not specifically use racist keywords? Should the platforms be profiling their users and carrying out proactive muting—"*We've been looking at your posts and we think you might be a racist, so we're going to take down your account for the duration of the Euros*".

Clearly, there are issues of online abuse, hate speech, and child grooming that need to be addressed and platforms have a part to play. I would not consider myself to be a defender of platforms, yet in these debates I keep on coming to the same question—"what more can they do?" and "what does 'enough' look like?" There was certainly nothing in the draft legislation, or the report, to bring answers to these questions. Just that this will be resolved in secondary

If we distil a lot of the reporting, clearly reinforced with the debate, the focus of blame lies in "algorithms". Algorithms have become the useful scapegoat for all manner of IT practices in recent times, and it has become an established part of political rhetoric regarding the regulation of technology. The then UK prime minister referred to "mutant algorithms" causing the issues that abound in terms of biased grades in examination results in 2020,[14] and this mistrust of algorithms remains an issue for our law makers

> … too long the major online service providers have been allowed to regard themselves as neutral platforms which are not responsible for the content that is created and shared by their users. Yet it is these algorithms which have enabled behaviours which would be challenged by the law in the physical world to thrive on the internet.

[14] https://www.bbc.co.uk/news/education-53923279 [Accessed October 2024]

And the subsequent debate on the report[15] is awash with rhetoric blaming the algorithms for the harms that occur online:

Suzanne Webb (Stourbridge) (Con):

> … let me explain about killer algorithms.
>
> An algorithm is a series of instructions telling a computer how to transform a set of facts about the world into useful information. My hon. Friend the Member for Gosport (Dame Caroline Dinenage) touched on the point that an algorithm can constantly recommend pictures of dogs to dog lovers like me, but the dark side is that it can also constantly recommend to a vulnerable teenager pictures of self-harm, suicide content, violent sexual pornography or unsolicited contact with adults they do not know, right the way through to more insidious harms that might be built up over time.

Dr Luke Evans (Bosworth) (Con):

> It is about algorithms. That is where I want the Bill to be stronger. In every meeting that I have had with TikTok, Instagram, Facebook or Snapchat—you name it—when I have asked about algorithms, they say, "We can't tell you more about it because it's commercially sensitive," but they are fundamentally what is driving us down the rabbit holes that the report rightly picks up on. How will we in this House determine what things look like if we do not understand what is driving them there in the first place? The horse has literally left the stables by the time we are picking up the pieces.

If we consider the final sentence of the quote from the report above, it makes clear that algorithms have "enabled behaviours" to thrive on the internet. This is simply not the case. We are reminded of the seminal work of Lessig, who stated "Code is Law" (Lessig, 2009):

> In real space we recognize how laws regulate—through constitutions, statutes, and other legal codes. In cyberspace we must understand how code regulates — how the software and hardware that make cyberspace what it is regulate cyberspace as it is. As William Mitchell puts it, this code is cyberspace's "law." Code is law.

---

[15] https://hansard.parliament.uk/Commons/2022-01-13/debates/1B9767E0-EF19-4D77-8C73-AADA64365D2C/DraftOnlineSafetyBillReport [Accessed October 2024]

As already stated above, there is nothing subjective about algorithms, they do exactly what they are told to do. While they are good at this, they are far less good at deciding whether a comment is racist, offensive, or abusive. Because the definitions for all of these are loosely defined and while an algorithm is outstanding at detecting an abusive keyword,[16] it is far less effective at interpreting natural language should the abuser choose not to use listed keywords. And it would be a problematic user experience should a platform be regularly triggering false positives and accusing innocent remarks as a racist. As Cathy O'Neill so eloquently documents (O'Neil, 2016), the algorithm is dumb, it is the coders and developers who introduce bias and problematic response into the code. Which, of course, is why platforms being able to demonstrate duty of care is a good thing,[17] as long as it is balanced and places reasonable expectations upon the development.

The Online Safety Act 2023 2023

Regardless of these debates and concerns, and in some cases concerns that the legislation would never see the light of day, in October 2023, after extensive debate and revisions, the bill finally received Royal Assent, becoming the Online Safety Act 2023 2023.

The UK Online Safety Act 2023 2023, it was claimed (Woods & Perrin, 2021), represented a significant legislative effort to enhance digital safety and regulate online content. The Act claimed to create a safer online environment for users, particularly children, by imposing stringent requirements on online platforms and services.

According to the UK government,[18] the Online Safety Act 2023 aims to create a safer digital environment by imposing stringent measures on online platforms and service providers to combat illegal and harmful content. The legislation mandates that platforms proactively prevent and

[16] Nevertheless, this is not a perfect system. As a resident of the South West of the UK, I was, until recently, frequently warned by Facebook's algorithms that posting comments about Plymouth Hoe could be deemed offensive. Unfortunately, it seems a keyword matching system listing "abusive" keywords considers Plymouth Hoe to be an offensive term for a Plymouth resident, rather than what it is, the delightful waterfront location within the city.

[17] I have taught ethics to Computer Science students for year. I usually start the lectures with: "Hands up if you'd get onto an aircraft for which you'd written the code". No one has ever put their hand up.

[18] https://www.gov.uk/guidance/a-guide-to-the-online-safety-bill

remove illegal content, such as child sexual exploitation, terrorism, hate crimes, and fraud, while also criminalizing content that promotes self-harm. Additionally, the Act emphasizes safeguarding children by requiring platforms to prevent access to harmful and age-inappropriate content, enforce age verification measures, and ensure age-appropriate user experiences.

To protect adults, the Act provides tools for users to control the content they see and interact with online, including filtering options for unverified users. Platforms must be transparent about their content moderation policies, publish regular reports, and adhere to their terms of service. The UK communications regulator, OFCOM, is empowered to enforce compliance, with the authority to impose substantial fines and take legal action against non-compliant platforms and senior managers.

- Regulated Services: The UK Online Safety Act 2023 2023 regulates user-to-user services (e.g. social media platforms) and search services that allow users to interact with content created by others. This includes platforms where user-generated content is shared or discussed. The Act also targets services that host pornographic content, which must implement specific measures to ensure children do not access this material.
- Extra-Territorial Application: The Act applies to any service that is accessible in the UK or targets UK users, regardless of the service provider's geographical location. This wide-reaching scope ensures that any digital service used by UK residents falls under the Act's regulations.
- Proactive Measures: Platforms are required to implement robust systems to prevent illegal content, such as child sexual abuse material, terrorism, and fraud, from appearing on their sites. They must also have mechanisms in place to swiftly remove any illegal content that does appear. This involves continuous monitoring and risk assessment to ensure that platforms are not being used for illegal activities.
- New Offences: The Act also introduces new criminal offences related to online activities, such as cyberflashing (sending unsolicited explicit images), strengthening intimate image abuse legislation (sharing private images without consent), and encouraging self-harm or suicide.
- Harmful Content: The Act mandates that platforms must protect children from content that, while not illegal, is harmful or age-inappropriate. This includes content promoting self-harm, eating

disorders, and bullying. Age assurance technologies, such as age verification and age estimation, are required to prevent children from accessing harmful content. Platforms must regularly assess the risks their services pose to children and implement measures to mitigate these risks.

- Age-Appropriate Experiences: Services must enforce age restrictions and ensure that children only have access to content that is appropriate for their age group. This includes providing clear terms of service that specify how age restrictions are enforced and ensuring these measures are applied consistently.

- Tools for Adults: The Act requires major platforms to provide tools that allow adult users to control their online experiences. This includes options to filter out content from unverified users and block harmful content, such as hate speech and content promoting self-harm. These tools must be easy to access and use, providing adults with greater control over what they see and whom they interact with online.

- Transparency: Platforms must be transparent about their content moderation policies and provide users with mechanisms to appeal content removal decisions. This transparency helps build trust and ensures that users understand how content is managed and moderated on the platforms they use.

- Regulatory Oversight: Ofcom, the UK communications regulator, is designated as the regulator for the Online Safety Act 2023. It has the authority to enforce compliance, issue penalties, and provide guidance. Ofcom will oversee the implementation of safety measures and ensure that platforms comply with their duties to protect users, especially children. At the time of writing Ofcom are still consulting on how they will implement regulation of the Online Safety Act 2023, but it is anticipated that they will, in due course, publish codes of practice and guidelines to help platforms meet their obligations.

- Penalties for Non-Compliance: Companies that fail to comply with the Act can face substantial fines, up to 10% of their global annual turnover or £18 million, whichever is greater. Ofcom also has the authority to take more severe actions, such as instructing payment providers and advertisers to cease working with non-compliant platforms, effectively restricting their operations in the UK.

However, if we are to reflect upon the ecosystem model presented in Chap. 1, we can clearly see that the expected stakeholder interactions take place in the macrosystem, a long way from the child, and with no engagement of the microsystem positioned closer to them. This is a significant point to explore later in this text, because it helps us understand why the policy direct continues to not resolve the issues young people face.

The evolution of the UK Online Safety Act 2023 2023 is a useful case study in the dynamic and often contentious relationship between technology, regulation, and societal values. This chapter so far has explored the journey from the early calls for online safety measures to the eventual enactment of the Act, emphasizing the significant role of political rhetoric and ideological motivations in shaping digital safety policies.

It's Like Déjà vu, Over and Over Again

The Act, if we are to believe the current government, represents a significant step forward in the UK's efforts to protect its citizens, particularly children, from harmful online content. By introducing a statutory duty of care, mandating robust age verification, and enhancing content moderation and transparency, the Act aims to create a safer online environment. However, as this chapter has demonstrated, the implementation of these measures is fraught with challenges, including the operational and financial burdens on platforms, the complexity of defining and measuring "harmful" content, and the ongoing tension between safety and freedom of expression.

The rhetoric that fuelled the legislative process reveals a persistent belief in the necessity of stringent regulation to counteract the perceived failures of self-regulation by tech platforms. This belief has been echoed globally, as evidenced by similar regulatory efforts in other jurisdictions. Yet, the practicalities of enforcing such regulations, especially in a rapidly evolving digital landscape, remain a significant hurdle. And the approach, as we have explored through this chapter, is resolutely fixed on technical intervention and platform liability, even though this has failed, at least twice, before, and, as explored in Chap. 1, there is case law emerging that highlights how problematic this platform liability and tough language approach is at tackling online harms.

Which does beg the question why is the new legislation more of the same? Certainly, there are developments in terms of the complexity of the platform liability (moving in the last twelve years from preventing youth access to pornography to the prevention of all harms on their platforms) but the stakeholder focus remains resolutely on industry. In order to try to understand this, there is some theory that helps us.

Path dependence (Kirk et al., 2007) is a concept that suggests once a particular course of action is taken, it becomes increasingly difficult to change direction due to the costs associated with switching paths, institutional inertia, and established practices. In the context of legislation, this means that once a certain type of law is enacted to address a social issue, subsequent attempts to address the same issue are likely to follow a similar approach. This is because policy makers, institutions, and stakeholders become accustomed to the existing framework, making it easier to build upon or modify existing laws rather than create entirely new approaches.

Path dependency persists even when there is no evidence that the current path is effective due to a confluence of factors that create formidable barriers to change (Barnett et al., 2015). These factors include institutional inertia, political considerations, cognitive biases, historical legacies, economic constraints, normative influences, and feedback mechanisms, all of which interlock to sustain the status quo. This relates somewhat to what is sometimes referred to as a "sunk cost fallacy" (McAfee et al., 2010).

Furthermore, the institutional concept of Isomorphism (Frumkin & Galaskiewicz, 2004) can be seen at play. Isomorphism refers to the process by which organizations (including legislative bodies) tend to become similar to each other over time due to various pressures such as coercive, mimetic, and normative isomorphism. In the legislative context, this can mean that policy makers repeatedly introduce similar types of legislation because they are influenced by the practices and norms of other institutions, jurisdictions, or historical precedents. This results in a homogenization of legislative approaches to similar social concerns (and we can already see considerable parallels between the Australian and UK legislation).

Coercive isomorphism (Othman et al., 2011) occurs when institutions adopt similar policies due to external pressures, such as laws, regulations, or mandates from higher authorities. In social policy, this can happen when national governments impose certain standards on local authorities or when international bodies set guidelines that member states must follow. Coercive influence can also come from stakeholders such as media organizations, non-governmental organizations (NGOs), and other influential actors in society. These stakeholders can exert pressure on institutions and policy makers to adopt certain policies from, for example, media influence, agenda setting, lobbying, and high-profile public cases that elicit a strong public reaction. As a result of this pressure, there is evidence in some areas of social policy that I have referred to in the past (Phippen, 2017) as examples of politician's syllogism:

The politician's syllogism, also known as the politician's logic, is a satirical form of reasoning attributed to decision-makers, especially in the political arena. It consists of three statements:

- We must do something.
- This is something.
- Therefore, we must do this.

This form of logic is often criticized for its lack of critical thinking and for being a knee-jerk reaction rather than a well-considered decision. The syllogism highlights how actions can be taken for the sake of appearing proactive, rather than because they are the best or most effective solutions. This flawed reasoning was popularized by the British television series "Yes, Minister" and its sequel "Yes, Prime Minister", where it was used to critique political decision-making processes. However, we can see evidence of this knee-jerk reaction in many areas of online safety policy such as the blocking of certain types of content or demands to circumvent encryption because there have been media cases where it is has been used by bad actors.

In this chapter, in our journey to better understand why online safety still seems to remain very poorly aligned with what young people are calling for, we have predominantly focussed upon a single stakeholder in the ecosystem—legislators and policy makers. In the next chapter we will attempt to understand why policy makers adopt these positions by seeing the role of the media, and its influence on policy makers and professionals. As we attempt to further unpick the interactions in the ecosystem and what happens if we are driven not by evidence but by knee-jerk reaction and moral panic, we once again observe historical lessons that have not been learned.

REFERENCES

Australian Government. (2021). *Online Safety Act 2023*. Accessed October 2024, from https://www.legislation.gov.au/C2021A00076/latest/text

Balkin, J. M. (2021). How to regulate (and not regulate) social media. *Journal of Free Speech Law, 1,* 71.

Barnett, J., Evans, L. S., Gross, C., Kiem, A. S., Kingsford, R. T., Palutikof, J. P., et al. (2015). From barriers to limits to climate change adaptation: Path dependency and the speed of change. *Ecology and Society, 20*(3).

Cates, M. (2024). *Regulating smartphones use for children.* Accessed October 2024, from https://www.miriamcates.org.uk/news/regulating-smartphone-use-children

Citron, D. K., & Wittes, B. (2018). The problem isn't just backpage: Revising Section 230 immunity. *Georgetown Law Technology Review, 2*(2), 453.

Deakin, S. F., Johnston, A. C., & Markesinis, B. S. (2012). *Markesinis & Deakin's Tort law* (7th ed., p. 99). Oxford University Press.

Ehrlich, P. (2002). Communications Decency Act Sec. 230. *Berkeley Technology Law Journal, 17*, 401.

European Union. (2022). *Regulation (EU) 2022/2065 of the European Parliament and of the Council of 19 October 2022 on a single market for digital services and amending Directive 2000/31/EC (Digital Services Act).* Accessed October 2024, from https://eur-lex.europa.eu/legal-content/EN/TXT/?uri=CELEX%3A32022R2065

Flonk, D. (2021). Emerging illiberal norms: Russia and China as promoters of internet content control. *International Affairs, 97*(6), 1925–1944.

Frumkin, P., & Galaskiewicz, J. (2004). Institutional isomorphism and public sector organizations. *Journal of Public Administration Research and Theory, 14*(3), 283–307.

Gillespie, T. (2017). Platforms are not intermediaries. *Georgetown Law Technology Review, 2*, 198.

Goldman, E. (2017). The ten most important Section 230 rulings. *Tulane Journal of Technology and Intellectual Property, 20*, 1.

Haidt, J. (2024). *The anxious generation: How the great rewiring of childhood is causing an epidemic of mental illness.* Random House.

Joint Committee on the Draft Online Safety Bill. (2021). *Draft online safety bill. Report of 2021–22 session.* Accessed October 2024, from https://committees.parliament.uk/publications/8206/documents/84092/default/

Kirk, E. A., Reeves, A. D., & Blackstock, K. L. (2007). Path dependency and the implementation of environmental regulation. *Environment and Planning. C, Government & Policy, 25*(2), 250–268.

Lessig, L. (2009). *Code: And other laws of cyberspace.* ReadHowYouWant.com

McAfee, R. P., Mialon, H. M., & Mialon, S. H. (2010). Do sunk costs matter? *Economic Inquiry, 48*(2), 323–336.

O'Neil, C. (2016). *Weapons of math destruction: How big data increases inequality and threatens democracy.* Crown.

Othman, S., Darus, F., & Arshad, R. (2011). The influence of coercive isomorphism on corporate social responsibility reporting and reputation. *Social Responsibility Journal, 7*(1), 119–135.

Phippen, A. (2017). *Children's online behaviour and safety: Policy and rights challenges.* Springer.

Review, B. (2008). *Safer children in a digital world: The report of the Bryon review.* Department for Children, Schools and Families.

UK Government. (2008). *Criminal Justice and Immigration Act 2008 Section 63.* Accessed July 2024, from http://www.legislation.gov.uk/ukpga/2008/4/section/63

UK Government. (2017a). *Making Britain the safety place in the world to be online.* Accessed October 2024, from https://www.gov.uk/government/news/making-britain-the-safest-place-in-the-world-to-be-online

UK Government. (2017b). *The Digital Economy Act 2017.* Accessed October 2024, from http://www.legislation.gov.uk/ukpga/2017/30/contents/enacted

UK Government. (2017c). *Internet safety strategy green paper.* Accessed October 2024, from https://assets.publishing.service.gov.uk/government/uploads/system/uploads/attachment_data/file/650949/Internet_Safety_Strategy_green_paper.pdf

UK Government. (2019a). *The online pornography (commercial basis) regulations 2019.* Accessed October 2024, from http://www.legislation.gov.uk/uksi/2019/23/pdfs/uksi_20190023_en.pdf

UK Government. (2019b). *Online harms white paper.* Accessed October 2024, from https://assets.publishing.service.gov.uk/government/uploads/system/uploads/attachment_data/file/793360/Online_Harms_White_Paper.pdf

UK Government. (2021). *Draft online safety bill.* Accessed October 2024, from https://assets.publishing.service.gov.uk/government/uploads/system/uploads/attachment_data/file/985033/Draft_Online_Safety_Bill_Bookmarked.pdf

UK Government. (2023). *Online Safety Act 2023.* Accessed July 2024, from https://www.legislation.gov.uk/ukpga/2023/50

Woods, L., & Perrin, W. (2021). *Obliging platforms to accept a duty of care* (pp. 93–109). Oxford University Press.

CHAPTER 3

Online Harms Moral Panics, the Last Five Years

Abstract This chapter explores the role of media-driven moral panics in shaping public perceptions of online safety and influencing policy responses to child online harms. Using high-profile cases such as the "Momo challenge" and concerns around grooming during COVID-19 lockdowns, the chapter illustrates how sensationalist media narratives amplify perceived threats to child safety, often leading to reactive rather than evidence-based policies. By examining historical moral panics, including the Satanic Panic of the 1980s, the text highlights recurring cycles of fear fuelled by exaggerated media coverage, public anxiety, and reactive policy making. Applying Stanley Cohen's framework, the chapter analyses how these moral panics contribute to a rhetoric of platform scapegoating and misplaced liability on tech companies. Emphasizing the need for critical media literacy and evidence-based approaches, the chapter argues for a balanced and informed response to online safety, advocating for strategies that prioritize actual risks and meaningful support for young people's digital experiences.

Keywords Moral panics • Media influence • Online safety • Platform scapegoating • Evidence-based policy

Following our analysis of policy makers' role in shaping the online safety agenda, this chapter turns to two additional influential forces: the media and its impact on the practice of those around the child. Operating closer to the child but still within the macrosystem, the media contribute significantly to public perceptions of online harms (and therefore policy makers, practitioners, and parents). Through high-profile cases like the "Momo suicide game" and concerns around COVID-related online grooming, we examine how sensationalist narratives—driven more by fear and conjecture than by evidence—have shaped public responses to youth online safety and help us understand the direction of travel with policy. Furthermore, these case studies also allow us to see how bias and unsubstantiated opinion can lead to moral panics, mirroring historical examples such as the 1980s Satanic Panic in the United States.

The analysis begins with a review of the cultural persistence of moral panics, which often hinge on adult anxieties around youth behaviour or the novelty and mistrust of emergent phenomena. We then consider how media narratives, public commentary, and stakeholder reactions amplify perceived risks, often resulting in a misplaced focus on platform scapegoating. Drawing on Cohen's moral panic framework, this chapter identifies the recurring steps by which exaggerated media reporting can spiral into widespread fear, leading authorities and professionals to respond with knee-jerk regulations rather than balanced solutions.

Ultimately, this chapter emphasizes the importance of critical media literacy and evidence-based responses in addressing online safety issues. By understanding the media's role in amplifying fears and the inclination of some professionals to favour prohibitionist over supportive measures, we explore the consequences of reactionary policies on young people's online experiences.

However, in this book one of the key theses is that we are failing in online safety policy because we believe it is new. As will be explored the belief that online harms are new because they happen online fails to appreciate a history of social policy that is often informed by moral panic, often informed by the media. There, we start with a history of moral panics hiding behind child safety to remind ourselves that while the internet may be new, moral panics are not.

SATANIC PANIC 2024

In the previous book I explored a lot of the media narratives around children's use of the internet and the potential harm that arises from stoking fear from a poorly informed position. I do not plan to do a similar deep dive into media discourse specifically here, but it is certainly not the case that things have improved. Over the course of writing this book there have been many media stories around online harms, for example

Children making AI-generated child abuse images, says charity[1]

Where the UK Safer Internet Centre (UKSIC) has reported that children are using Artificial Intelligence image generators to create indecent images of their peers. They stressed that despite their curiosity-driven actions, young people need to understand that such activities are illegal under UK law. The UKSIC called for a collaborative approach involving schools and parents to address this issue. Presumably by collectively telling young people they are breaking the law if they do this. Additionally, the article reported on AI "declothing" apps that had been misused to create fake nude images, highlighting a recent case in Spain,[2] which raised concerns about the increasing sophistication and misuse of AI technology.

Ofcom: Almost a quarter of kids aged 5-7 have smartphones[3]

The article stated that a new report (OFCOM, 2024) from the telecommunications regulator in the UK, Ofcom, showed that nearly a quarter of UK children aged 5–7 now own smartphones. The study also highlights an increase in social media and messaging app usage among young children, with nearly 40% using WhatsApp despite its minimum age requirement of 13. The article stated many children are using social media platforms like TikTok and Instagram despite being underage, often with parents' knowledge but insufficient oversight. It commented that parents struggle to enforce rules due to peer pressure and the perceived necessity of keeping children connected and safe, and highlighted a belief that parental enforcement of age restrictions appears to be diminishing, prompting Ofcom to call for the tech industry to do more to protect

---

[1] https://www.bbc.co.uk/news/technology-67521226 [Accessed October 2024]
[2] https://www.bbc.co.uk/news/world-europe-66877718 [Accessed October 2024]
[3] https://www.bbc.co.uk/news/technology-68838029 [Accessed October 2024]

children. One should note that at no point in the article did either the authors or contributors state why this was a bad thing, just that it should not happen.

Nine-year-olds added to malicious WhatsApp groups[4]

A BBC investigation found that children as young as nine were being added to malicious WhatsApp groups promoting self-harm, sexual violence, and racism. Northumbria Police warned thousands of parents after discovering widespread involvement of young children in these groups. Criticism was levelled at the platform provider, and said that despite WhatsApp lowering its minimum age from 16 to 13, the NSPCC criticized the lack of effective protections. They related concern to the death of Molly Russell in 2017, which was linked to harmful online content, to highlight the severe risks. The report stated that parents said they had difficulties in controlling their children's online activity, with some children continuing to receive disturbing messages even after leaving groups. The UK Prime Minister Rishi Sunak emphasize the need for stronger regulations under the Online Safety Act 2023. Critics had urged social media companies to *prioritize child safety over profits*. At no point in the article was there any discussion about parental intervention being needed to mitigate these risks, just that it was too complex for parents to manage therefore another stakeholder, far removed from the child, should.

These articles are typically representative of media reporting on online harms over the duration of writing this book. There are three key tropes to draw from the reporting:

1. Young people doing things that are illegal should be told its illegal as this will stop them doing it
2. Platforms are responsible for any harms, as it is too complex for parents to deal with
3. New duty of care legislation will stop this from happening

An underlying tone of all of these articles (and many others) is the sinister nature of the online world and the many harms that can be caused to young people. The use of extremely serious (but thankfully rarely

---

[4]https://www.bbc.co.uk/news/articles/cy0l4z8n1p9o [Accessed October 2024]

occurring) cases to illustrate these points reiterate the potential for significant harm.

The narrative that dominates this discourse is one of *platform scapegoating*—given that harms occur on these platforms they should be held responsible for allowing them to happen and should also prevent further harms from occurring. Back in the days where I made myself more available to the media to respond to online harms, stories of a typical scenario went something like this:

- A new online phenomenon has occurred, and young people are using a new piece of online technology.
- A journalist calls to ask what the harms would be for children using this.
- I respond by saying it seems to be, in general, just a form of communication and interaction using online technology.
- The journalist asks whether a child could be groomed/exposed to harmful content/abuse others on the technology and what can platforms do to stop it.
- I say possibly but there are many other situations where this would be the case and that while platforms have a role to play in providing routes for disclosure and to act upon those, other stakeholders (such as parents) have an important role to play too.
- Story is running saying "Expert says children are at risk and platforms do nothing".

This might be a reason why I do far less media unless I can carefully control the output.

For a long time, media stories that stoke moral panics and report on extreme cases generate more sales/clicks (Goode & Ben-Yehuda, 2010) and we can learn from history if we step back from online harms and look at other examples of this.

The Satanic Panic (Hughes, 2021) was a widespread moral panic in the United States during the 1980s and early 1990s, characterized by fear of widespread satanic ritual abuse (SRA) and the alleged presence of satanic cults involved in child abuse, murder, and other heinous acts. This phenomenon had deep social, cultural, and legal ramifications. The origins of the Satanic Panic could be traced back to the late 1970s (ibid.), when societal fears about the welfare of children (this is an important issue to bear in mind when we return to moral panics involving online technology) and concerns over rising crime rates began to intertwine with sensational media coverage and pseudo-scientific claims. Books like *Michelle Remembers* by Michelle Smith and her psychiatrist, Lawrence Pazder (Goodwin, 2018), played a pivotal role in igniting the panic. The book detailed supposed recovered memories of ritual abuse, despite lacking credible evidence and, as is typical in publishing and media output, its popularity spurred a wave of similar claims.

The panic gained significant traction in 1983 with the McMartin Preschool trial in California (Garven et al., 1998). The trial began after a parent accused childcare workers of sexually abusing her son. The case expanded as more children came forward, allegedly recounting bizarre and horrific stories of abuse. These testimonies were often obtained through suggestive interviewing techniques, which have since been discredited (ibid.). The trial, which lasted seven years and cost $15 million, ended with no convictions. Nonetheless, it highlighted and amplified the fear of widespread satanic abuse.

During this period, the media played a crucial role in perpetuating the panic. Talk shows, news programmes, and tabloid newspapers featured dramatic stories about satanic rituals and child abuse. Geraldo Rivera's 1988 television special, "Devil Worship: Exposing Satan's Underground" (Ellis, 2014) reached an audience of millions, further embedding these fears into the public consciousness. And these media portrayals often lacked critical scrutiny or alternative perspective, which presented allegations as facts, and therefore contributed to the hysteria.

Psychiatrists and social workers also played a significant role in the panic. The use of recovered memory therapy became widespread (Stocks, 1998), with therapists helping patients "recover" memories of abuse that often involved satanic rituals. These methods have since been criticized for implanting false memories in patients (Porter et al., 1999).

The panic had severe, real consequences in some cases. Numerous individuals were wrongfully accused and convicted based on dubious evidence and coerced testimonies. For instance, the West Memphis Three—teenagers Damien Echols, Jason Baldwin, and Jessie Misskelley—were convicted of murdering three boys in Arkansas in 1993. The prosecution alleged the murders were part of a satanic ritual, a theory that has since been debunked, leading to the release of the West Memphis Three in 2011 after new evidence emerged (Stidham et al., 2011).

Legal reforms and a more critical approach to accusations of abuse began to emerge in the late 1990s and early 2000s. The FBI's 1992 report, authored by Kenneth Lanning, concluded that there was no evidence to support claims of organized satanic ritual abuse. This report,[5] along with other studies and increasing scepticism, helped to dissipate the panic.

However, gaming phenomenon at the time got caught up with these panics, among them the role-playing game Dungeons & Dragons (D&D). This game, developed by Gary Gygax and Dave Arneson and first published in 1974, became a focal point for the anxieties and fears that characterized this period (Laycock, 2015).

Dungeons & Dragons is a fantasy role-playing game where players create characters and embark on imaginary adventures in a collaborative storytelling format. The game's use of mythical creatures, magic, and complex narratives involving good versus evil captured the imagination of many players. However, its popularity also attracted negative attention, particularly from conservative Christian groups and concerned parents who feared that the game's content could influence impressionable young minds (ibid.). Because the game was new and not something adults had experienced, it was believed to be risky and should be stopped (does that not sound familiar?).

The association between D&D and satanism began to emerge prominently in the early 1980s. Critics claimed that the game promoted occultism, witchcraft, and even demon worship. These fears were amplified by a few high-profile incidents. The 1979 disappearance of James Dallas Egbert III, a student at Michigan State University, was one such case (Waldron, 2005). Egbert, who played D&D, went missing and was later found to have run away due to personal issues unrelated to the game. However, the media sensationalized the connection, suggesting that D&D had played a role in his actions. This narrative was further propagated by author Rona Jaffe's 1981 book *Mazes and Monsters* (Jaffe, 2015) which fictionalized Egbert's story and was later adapted into a television movie.

Another significant incident was the suicide of Irving Pulling, a high school student in 1982 (Pasanen, 2017). His mother, Patricia Pulling, believed that D&D was directly responsible for her son's death. She founded Bothered About Dungeons & Dragons (BADD) and became a vocal critic of the game, appearing on talk shows and in media interviews. Patricia Pulling's activism contributed significantly to the public's perception of D&D as a dangerous influence (Cleary, 2022). Her claims,

---

[5] https://web.archive.org/web/20031025012607/http://www.pointnet.ca/media/igtaorca.pdf [Accessed October 2024]

although lacking scientific evidence, resonated with the fears of many parents during the Satanic Panic.

And the media played a substantial role in propagating the notion that D&D was linked to satanic practices. Television programmes and newspaper articles often featured dramatic and sensationalized stories about the game, presenting it as a gateway to the occult. This coverage was rarely balanced or well researched, and it amplified the panic by treating allegations as established facts.

Despite the hysteria, there was no credible evidence to support claims that D&D led to criminal behaviour or satanic worship. Studies conducted by psychologists and sociologists found no link between the game and harmful actions (Martin & Fine, 2017). In fact, many researchers noted the positive aspects of the game, such as its promotion of creativity, teamwork, and problem-solving skills.

By the late 1990s and early 2000s, the Satanic Panic began to subside, and with it, the scrutiny of Dungeons & Dragons. Public perception shifted as more people understood the game and recognized the baselessness of earlier accusations. Today, D&D enjoys widespread popularity and is recognized as a mainstream hobby, with its once-feared elements now seen as harmless components of imaginative play.

However, the legacy of the Satanic Panic persists, reflecting how societal fears can be amplified by media and professional authorities, leading to devastating consequences. The Harry Potter series by J.K. Rowling once reaching mainstream popularity after the publication of the first book in 1997 sparked controversy among certain conservative Christian groups, who argued that the books promoted witchcraft, the occult, and satanism to children (Soulliere, 2010).

Critics feared that the books' detailed depictions of spells, potions, and magical creatures could lead children to explore real-world occult practices (Buckley, 2017). This fear led to campaigns to remove the books from school libraries and reading lists in various countries, particularly in the United States. Religious leaders argued that the books glorified magic, contrary to biblical teachings, and undermined parental authority by promoting a worldview incompatible with Christianity. Once these concerns were in the wider public discourse psychological concerns also emerged (Taub & Servaty-Seib, 2008), with critics suggesting that immersing young readers in a magical world could desensitize them to the seriousness of occult practices.

Once again, over time, the panic surrounding Harry Potter diminished, and the books have become a part of mainstream children's literature. However, the controversy illustrates how cultural phenomena can become scapegoats in times of societal fear and underscores the importance of critical media engagement.

These examples serve as a cautionary tale about the dangers of moral panics, the importance of critical media consumption, and the need for rigorous standards in the criminal justice system. The episode underscores the vulnerability of society to mass hysteria and the profound impact it can have on individuals' lives.

This brief historical intervention is worthwhile when considering the current political and media (and therefore extending to other stakeholders) around children's use of online technology and the harms that they may cause. The stoking of panic and poorly informed opinion pieces and causations of the satanic panic can also be seen in some discourse around online harms.

Typically, from a theoretical perspective, I find that Stanley Cohen's work on moral panics, particularly his seminal book *Folk Devils and Moral Panics* (Cohen, 2011) even though it was written many years ago, has a profound influence on understanding these issues. Cohen introduced the concept of moral panics to describe the reaction of society to certain behaviours or groups that are perceived as a threat to social order. His analysis is crucial for understanding how media, public opinion, and authorities interact to amplify these perceived threats, often leading to significant social and political consequences.

Cohen defines a moral panic as a situation where a condition, episode, person, or group emerges to become defined as a threat to societal values and interests. This threat is then stylized and presented in a stereotypical fashion by the mass media, the moral barricades are manned by editors, bishops, politicians, and other right-thinking people. Socially accredited experts pronounce their diagnoses and solutions; ways of coping are evolved or (more often) resorted to, and the condition then disappears, submerges, or deteriorates and becomes more visible.

Cohen made it clear that moral panics are not new phenomena; they have occurred throughout history whenever a society has perceived a deviation from its norms as threatening. Cohen's work, however, provides a structured framework to understand the mechanisms and stages of such panics in the modern era. He emphasizes the role of the media in amplifying the perceived threat and shaping public perception, as well as the responses from authorities and the long-term consequences of these responses.

Cohen's analysis includes several historical examples of moral panics. One of the most famous cases he examined is the moral panic surrounding the Mods and Rockers in the 1960s in the United Kingdom (ibid.). These youth subcultures were involved in a series of highly publicized clashes that were portrayed by the media as a serious threat to social order. The sensationalized reporting led to public outcry and a strong response from authorities, including increased policing and calls for stricter regulations on youth behaviour.

Another notable example Cohen explores is the moral panic surrounding drug use in various societies, particularly during the "War on Drugs" era in the United States. The media played a crucial role in portraying drug users as dangerous criminals, leading to widespread public fear and support for harsh legal penalties. This panic resulted in significant changes to drug laws and enforcement practices, many of which continue to have profound social and racial implications.

In both cases the general media, and then policy, narrative has been one of prohibition—we need to stop this.

Cohen outlined five stages through which a moral panic progresses:

1. Emergence: This stage involves the identification of a problem by the media and other societal gatekeepers. The problem can be based on real or perceived events, and it is often characterized by the identification of a particular group (referred to by Cohen as "folk devils") as the source of the problem. These folk devils are depicted as a threat to societal norms and values. The emergence stage is crucial as it sets the stage for the ensuing panic by pinpointing the "enemy" that society must rally against.
2. Media Inventory: In this stage, the media's portrayal of the problem is critical. The media engages in sensational reporting, which exaggerates the scale and nature of the threat. This reporting often includes dramatic headlines, lurid details, and stereotypical images, which serve to magnify public concern. The media's role is not just passive reporting but active construction of the narrative that frames the issue in a particular light, often invoking fear and moral outrage.
3. Public Concern: As the media coverage intensifies, public anxiety and concern escalate. This stage is marked by widespread fear and anger, which are directed towards the identified folk devils. Public

opinion becomes increasingly polarized, with a growing consensus that something must be done to address the threat. It is at this point that policy makers often become involved as a reaction to the media hysteria and subsequent public outcry.

4. Response from Authorities: Authorities and policy makers respond to the heightened public concern by implementing measures to counteract the perceived threat. This response can include the introduction of new laws, the enhancement of policing efforts, and other forms of social control. The authorities' actions often serve to legitimize the panic and can have long-lasting implications. These responses are typically framed as necessary for the protection of societal values and the maintenance of social order.

5. Social Change: The final stage involves either a resolution of the panic or its evolution into new forms of social control. The measures taken by authorities may lead to a reduction in public concern, but the legacy of the panic can endure, influencing future policies and societal attitudes. In some cases, the identified folk devils may be marginalized or stigmatized for an extended period. The social change resulting from a moral panic can thus reshape the social landscape, sometimes in ways that reinforce existing power structures.

The work has a strong relevance to modern societal concerns where media plays an even more pervasive role in shaping public perception and Cohen's work offer insights into the mechanisms of social control and the potential for both harm and cohesion that can arise from moral panics. For example, we can see strong parallels with Cohen's moral panics in the 1970s and media and policy response to online safety concerns now.

As the internet becomes increasingly central to everyday life, concerns about online safety, in all its forms, often provoke strong reactions from the public, media, and, therefore, authorities. If we explore this through Cohen's framework:

1. Emergence: Online safety issues such as abuse, online predators, and privacy violations are identified as significant threats. This stage often begins with specific incidents that gain attention, such as a high-profile case of online harassment or significant harm to a child. These incidents highlight the potential dangers of digital interactions and trigger societal concern. The folk devils can be individuals

or groups like abusers but have also evolved to be the "uncaring" and "wanting to profit from children's misery" tech companies perceived to fail to prevent harms from occurring. These entities are framed as antagonists threatening the safety of internet users, especially vulnerable populations like children and teenagers.

2. Media Inventory: As highlighted above with three brief examples, the media plays a crucial role by extensively covering incidents related to online safety. Headlines and stories often focus on the most alarming aspects of these incidents, using dramatic language and imagery to capture attention. This sensational reporting amplifies the perceived threat and is rarely based in evidence. Social media further intensifies this process, as users share and comment on these stories, often adding their own fears and concerns (see below regarding the Momo case). The rapid spread of information (and misinformation) online can escalate the public's perception of the threat.

3. Public Concern: As media coverage continues, public anxiety about online safety grows. Parents, educators, and policy makers express increasing concern about the risks posed to children and the general public. Discussions about the dangers of the internet become widespread, leading to a heightened sense of urgency to address these issues. Public discourse often includes moral judgements about the behaviour of those involved in perpetuating online threats or in engaging in behaviour deemed unacceptable (see the AI nude fake images story above). There is a call for greater accountability and stricter measures to protect internet users as a result and the fear and moral outrage drive a demand for immediate action to mitigate these threats. Policy makers see the opportunity for public exposure as the moral guardian and engage with the media discourses.

4. Response from Authorities: Authorities respond to the public's concerns by proposing and implementing measures aimed at enhancing online safety (2012 can be seen as the starting point of currently platform liability legislative initiatives in the UK). This can include new laws to pressure tech companies to adopt stricter policies and technologies to protect users. Measures to improve online safety often involve increased monitoring of online activities (see the Safeguarding Dystopia). For instance, law enforcement agencies might enhance their capabilities to track and apprehend cybercriminals. Tech companies may also implement more rigorous content moderation practices to tackle "harmful" behaviours on their plat-

forms due to political pressure (i.e. "Do something or we will regulate").

5. Social Change: I would strongly argue that we have not yet got to this point, as new technology and behaviours emerge, we continue to bounce between one and four while losing sight of what we purport to do, which is to support young people to have positive online experiences. I would reflect on the fact that in the early twenty-first century when I was first discussing these issues with young people (Lacohee et al., 2006), their main calls were for better education and more supportive adults around them. This, as we will explore in Chap. 5, remains the case to this day. If there had been effective social change, we would have the needs of young people who have moved on. The fact they have not shown the failings of adult stakeholders and the lock into the moral panic cycle.

These stages can be explored with two examples below, both of which trigger panic and, certainly in one case, negative outcomes for young people, by professionals claiming to have the best interests of the child at the heart of what they do.

The Viral Digital Ghost Story

In 2019, in the final week of February (specifically February 25–March 2, 2019), the UK saw what we might regard as a "moral panic" emerge from both social media and traditional news outlets related to a phenomenon referred to as Momo. This was reportedly *another* "suicide game" online that was encouraging children to self-harm and kill themselves.

According to the popular wisdom, the "Momo challenge" placed a disturbing image (which is actually a photograph of a sculpture of an *ubume* produced by the artist Keisuke Aisawa[6] in 2016) in children's videos online. The image would "speak" to the viewer, giving them a mobile phone number for them to contact, which would then set up a series of "challenges" for the victim, which involved challenges to self-harm or instructions to commit suicide (Alderton, 2021). News reports claimed the challenge had been linked to the suicides of children in Argentina,

---

[6] https://www.instagram.com/p/BlQlfA2Biju/ [Accessed October 2024]

Mexico, and India.[7] Obviously, this was very worrying for anyone with children. However, it was also entirely fake.

We in the online safety community had been aware of Momo since 2018, most have ignored it for what it is—a hoax, simply a folk tale that has been taken up by various online trolls who wish to scare children by placing the image in, for example, videos of Peppa Pig, alongside a few poorly crafted messages. In the same way that "Rickrolling"[8] placed a video of the pop star Rick Astley in an unexpected link or video, this was simply a prank (albeit, in the case of Momo, an unpleasant one) done by meme creators to generate views, hits on their content, and possibly gain some notoriety by upsetting children along the way.

Therefore, it was something of a surprise to see it so significantly hit the headlines in late February 2019, and public consciousness with calls by celebrities, "online safety" companies, academics, police, schools, and the news media for social media providers (particularly YouTube) to do the responsible thing and control the spread of the challenge on their platforms. To YouTube's credit, they responded in a very factual and measured way:[9]

> Many of you have shared your concerns with us over the past few days about the Momo Challenge—we've been paying close attention to these reports. After much review, we've seen no recent evidence of videos promoting the Momo Challenge on YouTube.

This is certainly not the first time that such a digital ghost story has created a social media storm. The Blue Whale Challenge[10] had a near-identical modus operandi (although with this one the alleged "suicides" were occurring in Russian) which, on investigation, proved to have been entirely unfounded. We have also seen claims of causation when this is very difficult to prove.

In all three of these cases the spread of "awareness" was virtually identical—reporting, comment from "responsible" bodies, social media spread, public outcry, then more rational comment to calm the hysteria.

---

[7] https://www.thesun.co.uk/news/6926762/what-momo-suicide-game-whatsapp-deaths-uk-hoax/ [Accessed October 2024]

[8] https://en.wikipedia.org/wiki/Rickrolling [Accessed October 2024]

[9] https://support.google.com/youtube/thread/1917881?hl=en   [Accessed October 2024]

[10] https://en.wikipedia.org/wiki/Blue_Whale_Challenge [Accessed October 2024]

In the week of the Momo hype wave, there was a near-perfect storm of news coverage, celebrity social media commentary, and "online safety" organizations all wishing to become the main player in "solving" this crisis (which didn't exist). Perhaps the biggest trigger for the spike in interest last week came when the Police Service of Northern Ireland produced a press release that raised serious concerns about the potential harm the Momo challenge posed.[11] Highlights of this press release included:

> Whilst no official reports have been made to Police, we are aware of the so-called "Momo" challenge and are already liaising with other UK Police Services to try to identify the extent of the problem and to look for opportunities to deal with this issue.

> This extremely disturbing challenge conceals itself within other harmless looking games or videos played by children and when downloaded, it asks the user to communicate with "Momo" via popular messaging applications such as WhatsApp. It is at this point that children are threatened that they will be cursed or their family will be hurt if they do not self-harm.

> I am disgusted that a so-called game is targeting our young children and I would encourage parents to know what your children are looking at and who they are talking to.

This release, coming from a source of authority, legitimized the reporting from the more tabloid end of news outlets, and other stakeholders in child safeguarding then triggered a social media storm using these "authoritative" sources, which parents, concerned about their children's safety, then propagated further. Awareness-raising resources were provided by some "online safety" organizations talking about how to tackle the Momo challenge (which, I should reiterate, did not exist), and these resources were shared by concerned individuals on social media, therefore driving the Momo challenge further into the public consciousness. All of this resulted in many children being made aware of "Momo", and of course they then went off to search for it online. In a conversation I had with a concerned parent about Momo, I was made aware that in the case of one local primary school, the headteacher took the threat so seriously she called all the

---

[11] https://www.psni.police.uk/news/Latest-News/250219-psni-statement-regarding-momo-challenge/ [Accessed October 2024]

children from the school in for an assembly, where she told them they should not look for Momo because it was dangerous.

To summarize, the timeline of Momo Week went something like:

- February 25, 2019: PSNI send press release about their concerns around Momo.
- February 26, 2019: An organization who sell online safety services to schools tweets a "guide to Momo" to help "thousands of concerns schools and parents".
- February 27, 2019: Celebrities (including Kim Kardashian West) start commenting regarding their concerns about Momo on social media.

Towards the end of Momo Week (February 28, 2019–March 2, 2019), thankfully more responsible media reporting[12] caused the hype to die down and interest in Momo soon died down. However, its impact could be measured through data regarding searches in schools. A charity with whom I have worked for many years (discussed in far more detail in Chap. 4) work with service providers in schools and, therefore, could collect monitoring data on searches conducted by schools on their networks for the week of the study. Therefore, we were able to quantify searches for Momo by children at these schools over the course of the week. In total the data provided was captured from 2681 schools.

As we can see from the data below, searches specifically on Momo Week and strongly correlated between "awareness raising" and search interest in schools. While we cannot categorically state that all of these searches were performed by children and young people, this data is collected from the main school filters and monitors, whereas most staff would use staff machines that allow them more unrestricted internet access.

- February 25, 2019: 453
- February 26, 2019: 1332
- February 27, 2019: 5944
- February 28, 2019: 15,371
- March 1, 2019: 11,364

---

[12] https://www.theguardian.com/technology/2019/feb/28/viral-momo-challenge-is-a-malicious-hoax-say-charities [Accessed October 2024]

Overall, during Momo Week, Momo-related topics were searched for 34,464 times, the week before it was search for seventy-six times. So during Momo Week the searches related to Momo in these 2681 increased by approximately 45000%. And we can suggest that most of the alarm that resulted in young people searching for this phenomenon, which would result in them retrieving alarm images of the ubume sculpture, were driven by adults with a responsibility for the safeguarding of these young people.

COVID Lockdowns and Online Harms Denial

In April 2020, the NSPCC, the leading children's charity in the UK, published an article on their website stating:

> Lonely children are twice as likely to be groomed online

And within the article there was a:

> Heightened risk of sexual abuse during coronavirus lockdown ... The NCA knows from online chats that offenders are discussing opportunities to abuse children during the crisis and Europol has seen a surge in attempts by offenders to contact young people on social media.

At a similar time, a range of online safeguarding organizations and law enforcement agencies voiced similar concerns. For example, the Internet Watch Foundation raised concerns that:

> There are warnings that, with schools being forced to shut, there is an increased risk of children being groomed and coerced online.

The National Crime Agency stated that:

> the NCA also knows from online chat that offenders are discussing opportunities to abuse children during the Covid 19 crisis.

Interpol followed with a similar report which stated:

> Boredom may lead to increased risk-taking, including an increase in the taking and sharing of self-generated material.

Furthermore UNICEF put out an alert:

> In South Africa, the current lockdown may put children's privacy in danger as they spend more time online.

As with the Momo alerts, these highlighted all of the components of a moral panic agencies. And while, if one was to pick apart these statements, it was essentially conjecture, the panic remained—with so many reputable agencies raising concerns, this must be true.

It is easy to see how this conclusion is easily reached. Being online is an inherently risky → More time online increases the risk to children → Children have spent more time online during lockdown → Online grooming in the UK has increased.

However, while the logic can be followed, does this mean that it is true? Sadly, the measurement of this sort of activity is difficult. While Ministry of Justice data will provide charges and prosecutions, and Freedom of Information requests might elicit some useful information about law enforcement activity, and helpline data might show about calls expressing concern, there is no single measure for the prevalence of online child sexual abuse and exploitation.

Clearly there would be logical conjecture that increased time online presents increased opportunity for both victims and offenders. However, while this might result in more attempts, this does not necessarily mean that they are more successful.

By way of sanity check, I issued a Freedom of Information request on all English local authorities requesting a weekly breakdown of safeguarding disclosure, both in general and those specific to online abuse.

In the UK, a Freedom of Information (FOI) request allows individuals to access information held by public authorities. This process is governed by the Freedom of Information Act 2000 (UK Government, 2000), which aims to foster transparency and accountability within public sector organizations.

Under this Act, anyone can request information from a wide range of public authorities, including central and local government bodies, the NHS, state schools, and police forces. The scope of the Act covers all recorded information, such as documents, emails, meeting minutes, research, and datasets, regardless of format.

To make an FOI request, you must do so in writing. This includes sending an email or a letter, clearly describing the information you seek.

While there is no specific format required, the request should include your name and an address for correspondence, which can be an email address.

Once a request is received, the public authority is obligated to respond promptly and within twenty working days. They must confirm whether they hold the requested information and then provide it, unless an exemption applies. Some exemptions include concerns of national security, personal data protection, commercial interests, and information intended for future publication. If information is withheld, the authority must explain the reason.

When it comes to data held by public authorities which related to statutory data, this is an extremely useful tool to test claims made by said authorities or other stakeholders.

I have used these approaches in the past, for example, when exploring how the laws around teen sexting have been applied to the criminalization of young (Phippen & Bond, 2023). They are useful because publicly funded bodies are legally bound to respond within a twenty-day period, so data can be collected quickly and potentially in considerable volumes.

While, of course, reiterating the point we make above that fractured and incomplete datasets can rarely show causation, if we are to follow the logic that "COVID lockdown will cause more online grooming of children", we would, surely, expect this to result in safeguarding disclosures?

If we look in a little more detail at the findings from this data collection exercise, the authorities were asked two very specific question:

1. Please can you provide the number of child safeguarding referrals you have received, per week, per referrer (school, police, healthcare, private citizen, other) from WC 6/1/2020 to WC 7/6/2020?"
2. If possible, please can you provide the number of child safeguarding referrals you have received, per week, per referrer (school, police, healthcare, private citizen, other) from WC 6/1/2020 to WC 7/6/2020, where the safeguarding concern refers to online abuse?

In considering the data received, there were responses from sixty local authorities in total. While we won't repeat the raw data in this text, there are some telling responses that do highlight findings appropriate to our investigations.

While there was a great deal of regional variation with disclosures, some basic statistics show a clear picture:

- Average number of disclosures per week pre-lockdown: 131
- Average number of disclosures per week during lockdown: 104
- Of the sixty authorities who responded, four saw an increase in disclosures during lockdown, and fifty-six saw a reduction.
- Overall lockdown disclosures were 78.2% if what would be expected per week before the lockdown.

Of course, there is an argument that disclosures will drop because schools are not seeing students face to face during this period and, therefore, would be less aware of safeguarding concerns. However, pre-lockdown, safeguarding referrals from schools accounted for less than 20% of referrals. While referrals from schools did decrease during lockdown, they did not cease entirely, as schools were still engaged with students during the lockdown period. Taken together with the decreased overall figures for referrals, this suggests that there is little evidence for an increase in safeguarding concern for young people during the lockdown period.

Furthermore, most local authorities responded to say that online abuse was not an explicit category that they were statutorily expected to record and, therefore, they did not.

As one local authority replied:

We have no statutory expectation from the Department for Education to hold this information.

Which does beg the question—how can we possibly know if online abuse has risen during lockdown given it is not recorded by those with a duty to keep record of safeguarding incidents? It is also, if we are in reflective mood, an indicator of the importance of statutory guidance to stakeholders in collecting data around online harms. It would seem from this response that if they are not asked to do it by a government department, they will not do it. Regardless of how useful that might be in contributing to evidence around young people's online safety risks.

Of course, the data from the Freedom of Information responses did not let us explore the context; this is simply data collected by local authorities on the safeguarding concerns of citizens. However, we would assume, if young people were being subject to more online abuse because of being online more, we would equally expect to see an increase in disclosures. The fact we did not and saw, in fact, in most local authorities, a significant drop in disclosures would challenge the popular mythology around the online harms threat that lockdown caused. Nevertheless, there were many stakeholders who believed it was their duty to disclose this information in the public domain, regardless of evidence to support claims, and regardless of the potential panic in the home these (unqualified) statements might cause.

Subsequent interviews with teachers and safeguarding leads in schools have further underpinned the view that, regardless of the rhetoric, there was little evidence that there were higher instances of online sexual abuse of children. Most teachers expressed the view that this was conjecture, rather than fact-based, and many passed observations about the challenges they faced in their settings when parents respond to this sort of rhetoric and expect schools to address concerns that have no basis in fact.

I also paraphrase a response from a 17-year-old young man I worked with around reactions to lockdown and online risk:

> I'm spending 8 hours a day online for school, I don't want to spend the evenings talking to pedos.

An illustration that young people develop risk mitigation strategies and that engaging in a behaviour that potentially carries some risk (such as going online in a place where people with a sexual interest in children might lurk, for example, multiplayer games and social media platforms) does not always equate to an experience of unwanted behaviour or criminal activity.

Conclusions

In this chapter, we have examined the influential role that media and professional responses play in shaping public perceptions of online harms. By analysing recent moral panics such as the Momo suicide game and COVID-19 online grooming fears, we have illustrated how bias and opinion can sometimes overshadow evidence-based approaches and how stakeholder response can sometimes be less than constructive.

The Momo case highlighted how a viral hoax can spiral into a moral panic, driven by sensationalist media coverage and amplified by celebrities and well-meaning but misinformed authorities. Despite the lack of concrete evidence, the widespread panic led to unnecessary fear and actions among parents and educators.

Similarly, the fears about increased online grooming during COVID-19 lockdowns were largely speculative. Our analysis showed that, contrary to the alarming predictions, there was no significant increase in safeguarding disclosures during this period. This underscores the need for a cautious and evidence-based approach when responding to such concerns.

Drawing parallels with the 1980s and 1990s Satanic Panic in the United States, we see a recurring cycle of fear and moral outrage driven by sensational media reports and unsupported claims. Stanley Cohen's framework on moral panics provides a useful lens to understand these dynamics, highlighting the stages from emergence to media amplification, public concern, authority response, and eventual social change.

In conclusion, this chapter advocates for an evidence-based approach to dealing with online harms. It stresses the importance of critical media consumption by all stakeholders around the child and the need for rigorous standards in both policy and media responses. By moving away from panic-driven measures and focusing on data and evidence, we can better protect young people and create a safer online environment. This balanced approach is essential for fostering informed and effective strategies in addressing the complex challenges of the digital age.

Furthermore, there is evidence in this analysis of stakeholders more concerned with media coverage and hero complex motivations to be the "saviour" of children in online spaces, and an iteration of finger pointing between stakeholders around who should be the one who resolves these issues, ultimately ending in a scapegoating of industry as the ones who have to ensure no child comes to any harm on their platforms while ignoring the role of others in supporting young people. Nevertheless, when considering where we are in 2024 compared to where we were in 2017, there is certainly a lot more rhetoric, and far more regulation and legislation. However, we need to consider whether, because of this, there are better outcomes for young people. In the next two chapters we will explore the microsystems—those stakeholders closer to the young people, and young people themselves, in considering whether the ecosystem is working for young people, or whether the swirl of activity in the macrosystem does little to improve outcomes for young people or connect with the microsystems.

References

Alderton, Z. (2021). The Momo challenge: Exploring the emergence of a major online Demonic Hoax. *Journal for the Academic Study of Religion, 34*(2).

Buckley, C. (2017). 'Do panic. They're coming': Remaking the weird in contemporary children's fiction. In *New directions in children's gothic* (pp. 16–31). Routledge.

Cleary, S. (2022). Better the devil you know: The myth of harm and the satanic panic. *Gothic Studies, 24*(2), 167–184.

Cohen, S. (2011). *Folk devils and moral panics*. Routledge.

Ellis, B. (2014). *Raising the devil: Satanism, new religions, and the media*. University Press of Kentucky.

Garven, S., Wood, J. M., Malpass, R. S., & Shaw, J. S., III. (1998). More than suggestion: The effect of interviewing techniques from the McMartin Preschool case. *Journal of Applied Psychology, 83*(3), 347.

Goode, E., & Ben-Yehuda, N. (2010). *Moral panics: The social construction of deviance*. John Wiley & Sons.

Goodwin, M. (2018). They couldn't get my soul: Recovered memories, ritual abuse, and the specter (s) of religious difference. *Studies in Religion/Sciences Religieuses, 47*(2), 280–298.

Hughes, S. A. (2021). *American tabloid media and the Satanic panic, 1970–2000*. Palgrave Macmillan.

Jaffe, R. (2015). *Mazes and monsters: A novel*. Open Road Media.

Lacohée, H., Phippen, A. D., & Furnell, S. M. (2006). Risk and restitution: Assessing how users establish online trust. *Computers & Security, 25*(7), 486–493.

Laycock, J. P. (2015). *Dangerous games: What the moral panic over role-playing games says about play, religion, and imagined worlds*. University of California Press.

Martin, D., & Fine, G. A. (2017). Satanic cults, satanic play: is "Dungeons & Dragons" a breeding ground for the devil? In *The satanism scare* (pp. 107–124). Routledge.

OFCOM. (2024). *Children's media literacy report 2024*. Accessed October 2024, from https://www.ofcom.org.uk/siteassets/resources/documents/research-and-data/media-literacy-research/children/children-media-use-and-attitudes-2024/childrens-media-literacy-report-2024.pdf

Pasanen, T. (2017). *Beyond the pale: Gaming controversies and moral panics as rites of passage*. Doctoral dissertation, University of Jyväskylä.

Phippen, A., & Bond, E. (2023). *Policing teen sexting – Supporting children's rights while applying the law*. Palgrave Macmillan.

Porter, S., Yuille, J. C., & Lehman, D. R. (1999). The nature of real, implanted, and fabricated memories for emotional childhood events: Implications for the recovered memory debate. *Law and Human Behavior, 23*, 517–537.

Soulliere, D. M. (2010). Much ado about Harry: Harry Potter and the creation of a moral panic. *The Journal of Religion and Popular Culture, 22*(1), 6–6.

Stidham, D., Fitzgerald, H., & Baldwin, J. (2011). Satanic panic and defending the West Memphis three: How cultural differences can play a major role in criminal cases. *University of Memphis Law Review, 42*, 1061.

Stocks, J. T. (1998). Recovered memory therapy: A dubious practice technique. *Social Work, 43*(5), 423–436.

Taub, D. J., & Servaty-Seib, H. L. (2008). Controversial content: Is Harry Potter harmful to children? In *Critical perspectives on Harry Potter* (pp. 25–44). Routledge.

UK Government. (2000). *Freedom of Information Act 2000.* Accessed October 2024, from https://www.legislation.gov.uk/ukpga/2000/36/contents

Waldron, D. (2005). Role-playing games and the Christian right: Community formation in response to a moral panic. *The Journal of Religion and Popular Culture, 9*(1), 3–3.

CHAPTER 4

Online Safety Policy and Practice—Exploring the Microsystems

Abstract This chapter examines the translation of national online safety policies into practical implementation within English schools, using the 360 Degree Safe and ProjectEVOLVE platforms as key datasets. Focusing on statutory responsibilities, it reveals a divide between the clear guidance issued by the Department for Education and actual practices, particularly in staff training and community engagement. The analysis shows a primary focus on simple topics like online relationships and self-image within primary schools, with a notable lack of attention to complex areas such as privacy and security, especially in secondary settings. This discrepancy highlights the inconsistency in online safety education across school stages and raises concerns about the robustness of current practices. The chapter argues that without comprehensive digital literacy education, the goals of national policies remain unmet, underscoring the need for balanced, evidence-based online safety initiatives that actively involve all stakeholders and address students' evolving needs.

Keywords Online safety implementation • Digital literacy education • School safeguarding policies • Stakeholder engagement • Policy-practice gap

© The Author(s), under exclusive license to Springer Nature Switzerland AG 2025
A. Phippen, *Policy and Rights Challenges in Children's Online Behaviour and Safety, 2017–2023*,
https://doi.org/10.1007/978-3-031-80286-7_4

In this chapter we move from exploring the macrosystems and the policy direction that has resulted in the Online Safety Act 2023, to exploring in far more detail what is occurring in exo- and microsystems within the ecosystem and whether what is purported to being tackled in the macrosystem transfers into the systems that are closer to young people, and will therefore have a more real impact upon their safeguarding. Specifically, in this and the next chapter we draw upon datasets that help us understand what is happening in schools within England, what education is being delivered and then, perhaps most importantly, what young people are telling us about their own online behaviours and worries. The data being drawn upon in these two chapters is significant and, in contrast to the ethnographic nature of discussions in the first two chapters, heavily quantitative. This is deliberate and aims to show the gulf between what policy makers claim needs to be tackled in keeping children safe online (and their claims of evidence for this), informed in the main by moral panic stoked by the media, and the reality of experiences for young people in learning about online risks and how to mitigate them. By presenting this, we develop the argument that there is a lot of evidence to draw upon, should policy makers wish to look.

Transforming Education Policy into Practice

Within England, the key statutory instrument related to safeguarding is the Department for Education's Keeping Children Safe in Education document (Department for Education, 2023) which instructs schools on all of their statutory duties related to the safeguarding of children and young people in their care. The document receives regular updates, and the statutory demands evolve with these updates. Online safety was first introduced as a distinct topic in the mid-2010s, its coverage in the guidance varies from year to year.

In the most up-to-date version of the document, there are several statutory expectations placed on schools related to online safety:

- Schools are required to develop and implement robust online safety policies. These policies should address the safe use of the internet, social media, and other digital technologies, that are understood by staff, students, and parents. This whole-school approach should emphasize that online safety is everyone's responsibility.

- Education and training are key components of the guidance. Staff should receive regular and updated training on online safety issues and learn how to identify and respond to potential online harms. For students, online safety education should be woven into the curriculum, equipping them with the knowledge to navigate the digital world safely. Schools should also engage parents, providing them with the information and guidance needed to support their children's online safety at home.
- To protect students from harmful online content, schools are required to have *appropriate* filters and monitoring systems in place. These systems should be regularly reviewed and adjusted to ensure they are effective without unnecessarily restricting learning opportunities.
- Clear procedures for reporting and managing online safety incidents are considered essential. Schools must have established mechanisms for reporting concerns, ensuring that students know who to turn to and what steps will be taken in response, ensuring that affected students receive the help they need.
- Recognizing that peer-on-peer abuse can occur online, the guidance emphasizes the need for schools to address such issues within their safeguarding policies. Similarly, the prevention and response to online bullying are highlighted, with schools required to educate students about the impact of online abuse and establish clear procedures for handling incidents.
- Schools are encouraged to collaborate with external agencies, such as the police and children's social care, to effectively address online safety issues and incidents. The guidance provides information and resources to help schools enhance their online safety practices.

Given this statutory guidance, one might assume that online safety policy and practice is well embedded into schools, and this is a stakeholder with whom we should not be concerned. However, our conversations with young people (see the next chapter) clearly show that this is not the case. It would seem, when one reflects upon the guidance, that while it is clear on the sorts of things a setting should be doing, such as having a policy, delivering education, providing training and ensuring scrutiny from governing bodies, what the guidance does not do (and nor should a regulatory document) is tell the schools how to do it. Therefore, it is down to schools, or their academy trust[1] to ensure they fulfil their statutory duties. Outside of the governing body, the key influencer on senior leaders to fulfil their duties is the school's inspectorate—Ofsted.

Ofsted, short for the Office for Standards in Education, Children's Services and Skills, is a non-ministerial department of the UK government that is responsible for inspecting a range of educational institutions, including state schools, some independent schools, and academies, as well as childcare, adoption and fostering agencies, and adult learning and skills providers. The primary purpose of Ofsted is to ensure that these institutions maintain high standards of education, care, and services, and to provide accountability through public reporting.

The key mechanisms for assessing starts are inspections and the subsequent inspection reports. Ofsted conducts regular inspections of schools and other educational institutions to assess their performance. These inspections are designed to ensure that institutions meet national standards. After inspection Ofsted publishes detailed reports on the institutions it inspects. These reports are made available to the public and are expected to provide information to stakeholders such as parents, students, staff, and the wider education community and reports on areas of strength and areas needing improvement.

However, while the current Ofsted inspection handbook makes it clear that inspection related to safeguarding can cover all aspects of Keeping Children Safe in Education, there are no explicit mentions of online safety in the current inspection handbook (OFSTED, 2024).

Therefore, while statutory guidance exists, and expectations are clear, there is a risk that, among the many other duties with the documentation, online safety might not be a priority, and similarly given what can be covered in an inspection, it might be that online safety is not covered.

In order to explore this further, and to show a far clearer picture of online safety policy and practice in schools, the remainder of this chapter explores two large datasets: the 360 Degree Safe dataset, which collects evidence on the practices of school who use a self-review tool to benchmark their performance in online safety (currently used in over 15,000

---

[1] The Academies Act 2010 provided a legal framework for groups of schools to form and operate as multi-academy trusts. A Multi-Academy Trust (MAT) is an organizational structure where multiple academies (state-funded schools that are independent of local authority control) are managed and overseen by a single governing body. This governing body, known as the board of trustees, is responsible for the strategic oversight, financial management, and overall performance of all the academies within the trust.

schools), and the ProjectEVOLVE dataset, drawing data from an online safety education platform that provides teaching resources and assessment frameworks at all levels of education in English schools, currently used by over 40,000 teachers.

In this detailed quantitative exploration, we can show that while there are some good areas of practice in schools, many, such as staff training, governor awareness and reach to the wider school community are still lacking. And drawing from the EVOLVE database we can see the nature of classes around online safety which, in turn, reflect what teachers are comfortable to deliver (bearing in mind there is little defined curriculum in England, Keeping Children Safe in Education simply mandates the online safety education should be delivered).

In exploring this data, we can see many policy challenges, such as the drop off in teaching after primary school, the lack of coverage of technical aspects of safety and risk mitigation, teachers delivering areas with which they are more comfortable (such as relationships and identity) and significant knowledge gaps around risk mitigation. As will be illustrated in this exploration, the data strongly conflicts with the policy belief that, due to statutory guidance and inspection, online safety is delivered and practiced in a consistent manner in schools. As such, it is a strong illustration that regulation does not necessarily result in effective implementation.

360 Degree Safe

The 360 Degree Safe was launched by SWGfL in November 2009 to allow schools to evaluate their own online safety provision; benchmark that provision against others; identify and prioritize areas for improvement and find advice and support to move forward. There are versions of the tool used in schools in England, Northern Ireland, Scotland, and Wales.[2] However, for this analysis we will focus on the largest database, which is English schools.

The 360 Degree Safe tool defines twenty-one aspects of online safety (Table 4.1):

For each of these aspects of the school is invited to rate their practice based upon five levels, generally defined as (Table 4.2):

---

[2] There are three versions of the tool available - 360safe.org.uk, used in England, 360safe-cymru.org.uk, used in Wales and 360safescotland.org.uk, used in Scotland

Table 4.1   360 Degree Safe aspect definitions

Acceptable use	How a school communicates its expectations for acceptable use of technology and the steps towards successfully implementing them in a school. This is supported by evidence of users' awareness of their responsibilities.
Agencies	How the school communicates and shares best practice with the wider community including local people, agencies, and organizations.
Contribution of young people	How the school maximizes the potential of young people's knowledge and skills in shaping online safety strategy for the school community and how this contributes positively to the personal development of young people.
Data security	Describes the school's compliance with Data Protection legislation and how it manages personal data. It describes the ability of the school to effectively control practice through the implementation of policy, procedure, and education of all users from administration to curriculum use.
Digital and video images	How the school manages the use and publication of digital and video images in relation to the requirements of the Data Protection Act 2018.
Families	How the school educates and informs parents and carers on issues relating to online safety, including support for establishing effective online safety strategies for the family.
Filtering	A school's ability to manage access to content across its systems for all users.
Governors	The school's provision for the online safety education of Governors to support them in the execution of their role.
Impact of online safety policy and practice	The effectiveness of a school's online safety strategy; the evidence used to evaluate impact and how that shapes improvements in policy and practice.
Mobile technology	The benefits and challenges of mobile technologies. This includes not only school provided technology, but also personal technology
Monitoring	How a school monitors internet and network use and how it is alerted to breaches of the acceptable use policy and safeguards individuals at risk of harm.
Online publishing	How the school, through its online publishing: reduces risk, celebrates success, and promotes effective online safety.
Online safety education programme	How the school builds resilience in its pupils/students through an effective online safety education programme, that may be planned discretely and/or through other areas of the curriculum.

(continued)

Table 4.1 (continued)

Online safety group	How the school manages and informs their online safety strategy, involving a group with wide representation that builds sustainability and ownership.
Online safety policy	Effective online safety policy; its relevance to current social and education developments; its alignment with other relevant school policies and the extent to which it is embedded in practice.
Online safety responsibilities	Describes the roles of those responsible for the school's online safety strategy including senior leaders and governors/directors.
Professional standards	How staff use of online communication technology complies with legal requirements, both school policy and professional standards.
Reporting and responding	The routes and mechanisms the school provides for its community to report abuse and misuse and its effective management.
Social media	The school's use of social media to educate, communicate, and inform. It also considers how the school can educate all users about responsible use of social media as part of the wider online safety strategy.
Staff	The effectiveness of the school's online safety staff development programme and how it prepares and empowers staff to educate and intervene in issues when they arise.
Technical security	The ability of the school to ensure reasonable duty of care regarding the technical and physical security of and access to school networks and devices to protect the school and its users.

Table 4.2 360 Degree Safe levels

Level 5	There is little or nothing in place
Level 4	Policy and practice are being developed
Level 3	Basic online safety policy and practice
Level 2	Policy and practice are coherent
Level 1	Policy and practice are aspirational

As well as generic definitions, for each aspect, the levels in documentation provided to the school have clear descriptors to allow the school to make an informed judgement.

This analysis is based on data collected up to May 2024. The tool allows schools to perform the self-review at their own pace, it is not necessary for them to complete twenty-one aspects before using the tool for improvement. As each aspect in the database is analysed independently, the tool collects all responses from each aspect regardless of whether an institution has completed a full review. However, a breakdown of accounts shows that over **6000** schools now have a full profile. The difference between total

Table 4.3 Total 360 Degree Safe accounts

Total accounts	17,277
Embarked on review	9046
Full profiles	6024

Table 4.4 School stages

Primary	8873
Secondary	2233
Not applicable	1670
All-through	67
16 plus	89
Nursery	44

accounts and engaged accounts is that there are several test accounts and historical accounts no longer used. For this analysis we draw from engaged accounts (Table 4.3):

The majority of the schools that have started their self-review are from the primary setting, which is unsurprising given the number of primary to secondary schools in England.[3] There are also several establishments who are defined as "not applicable", that don't easily fit into an easy definition of phase (e.g. local authorities, pupil referral units, community special schools, and independents) (Table 4.4).

Average Ratings

A top line measure of online safety performance in English schools is the overall average rating of each aspect.

Each aspect can be rated by the self-reviewing establishments on a progressive maturity scale from 5 (lowest rating) and 1 (highest). In all cases, analysis of the aspect ratings shows an across establishment maximum rating of 1 and minimum of 5.

In considering how we classify the performance of each aspect in the database, the baseline rating for practice or policy for a given aspect is 3—which means, as detailed above, that they have achieved "Basic online safety policy and practice". Therefore, in order to categorize aspect

---

[3] According the UK government data (https://explore-education-statistics.service.gov.uk/find-statistics/school-pupils-and-their-characteristics) there are 16,791 primary schools and 4190 secondary schools, so approximately half of the schools in England use the tool.

Table 4.5 Aspect averages

Aspect	Rating
Filtering	2.136
Online safety policy	2.171
Monitoring	2.233
Acceptable use	2.239
Digital and video images	2.246
Professional standards	2.368
Mobile technology	2.464
Online safety education programme	2.498
Online safety responsibilities	2.531
Online publishing	2.599
Social media	2.599
Technical security	2.678
Reporting and responding	2.714
Families	2.772
Data security	2.810
Staff	2.989
Contribution of young people	3.002
Online safety group	3.185
Impact of online safety policy and practice	3.205
Governors	3.208
Agencies	3.431

performance, we break them down as (from strongest to weakest) (Table 4.5):

If we consider the 360 Degree Safe definitions from the strongest five aspects (Table 4.6):

We can see that both broad policy and technical measures are generally sound in the schools returning self-review with the tool.

However, if we consider the weakest aspects (Table 4.7):

We can see that the aspects that require a longer-term resource investment relate to training or require broader stakeholder buy-in tend to be weaker. Specifically, they relate to stakeholder development and engagement across the ecosystem.

Standard Deviation

A further measure of the national picture can be taken by considering the standard deviation of each aspect. Therefore, for aspects with a low

Table 4.6 Strongest aspects

Acceptable use	How a school communicates its expectations for acceptable use of technology and the steps towards successfully implementing them in a school. This is supported by evidence of users' awareness of their responsibilities.
Digital and video images	How the school manages the use and publication of digital and video images in relation to the requirements of the Data Protection Act 2018
Filtering	A school's ability to manage access to content across its systems for all users.
Monitoring	How a school monitors internet and network use and how it is alerted to breaches of the acceptable use policy and safeguards individuals at risk of harm.
Online safety policy	Effective online safety policy; its relevance to current social and education developments; its alignment with other relevant school policies and the extent to which it is embedded in practice.

Table 4.7 Weakest aspects

Contribution of young people	How the school maximizes the potential of young people's knowledge and skills in shaping online safety strategy for the school community and how this contributes positively to the personal development of young people.
Agencies	How the school communicates and shares best practice with the wider community including local people, agencies, and organizations.
Governors	The school's provision for the online safety education of Governors to support them in the execution of their role.
Impact of online safety policy and practice	The effectiveness of a school's online safety strategy; the evidence used to evaluate impact and how that shapes improvements in policy and practice.
Online safety group	How the school manages and informs their online safety strategy, involving a group with wide representation that builds sustainability and ownership.
Staff	The effectiveness of the school's online safety staff development programme and how it prepares and empowers staff to educate and intervene in issues when they arise.

standard deviation, most institutions will more closely fit around the average value than those with a broad deviation. Whereas a broader deviation would suggest greater diversity of practice (Table 4.8).

If we rate different standard deviation values as (Table 4.9):

If we initially explore the strongest aspects (Table 4.10):

Table 4.8 Aspect standard deviations

	Std Dev
Filtering	0.853
Monitoring	0.859
Online safety policy	0.869
Families	0.884
Online safety education programme	0.887
Acceptable use	0.899
Staff	0.990
Data security	0.994
Digital and video images	1.005
Agencies	1.023
Impact of online safety policy and practice	1.035
Technical security	1.039
Online safety responsibilities	1.042
Contribution of young people	1.057
Governors	1.081
Mobile technology	1.081
Social media	1.090
Online publishing	1.091
Reporting and responding	1.105
Professional standards	1.148
Online safety group	1.269

Table 4.9 Standard deviation ranges

Aspect standard deviation score	Rating
Less than 0.99	Narrow
Between 1–1.19	Typical
1.2 or higher	Broad

Table 4.10 Strongest aspect averages and standard deviations

Aspect	Average	Standard deviation
Filtering	2.136	Narrow
Online safety policy	2.171	Narrow
Monitoring	2.233	Narrow
Acceptable use	2.239	Narrow
Digital and video images	2.246	Typical

Table 4.11   Weakest aspect averages and standard deviations

Aspect	Average	Standard deviation
Agencies	3.431	Typical
Governors	3.208	Typical
Impact of online safety policy and practice	3.205	Typical
Online safety group	3.185	Broad
Contribution of young people	3.002	Typical
Staff	2.99	Narrow

Therefore, for the majority of the strongest aspects, a narrow deviation means that this practice in consistent across most schools in the dataset.

However, there is a different picture for those aspects that are cause for concern (Table 4.11):

For weaker aspects, having a narrow deviation means that there is consistency in weakness across the dataset, for example, we can see that Staff (the training of staff around online safety) is both cause for concern and narrow. Agencies (working with other stakeholders) is the weakest in the data recorded, and has a typical standard deviation, so we can be confident in most settings schools are not implementing this aspect effectively.

Aspect Frequency Distribution

As a final measure of assessing the performance of schools in the database, we can look at the distribution of levels per aspect—this means per aspect considering the proportion of schools that are rated level 1, level 2, and so on. Given that level 3 is considered "basic" or simply meeting the fundamental requirements of the aspect, we can consider those reporting level 4 or 5 being below these requirements and is a useful ranking (Table 4.12).

If we reflect upon the statutory expectations for schools in England, we can see that policy does not necessarily change into practice. Almost half of all schools do not engage with external stakeholders around online safety, and just over a third have no staff training, *even though this is a statutory requirement*. Perhaps a bigger concern, given their role in providing challenge to the senior team regarding online safety, the fact that almost half of schools provide no training for their board means it is unlikely they will receive sufficient challenge. Furthermore, even though

Table 4.12   Aspect frequency-level distributions

	1 (%)	2 (%)	3 (%)	4 (%)	5 (%)	Below threshold for basic practice (%)
Acceptable use	20.4	45.2	25.9	7.4	1.2	8.6
Agencies	2.4	16.4	33.5	31.2	16.5	47.8
Contribution of young people	5.6	31.6	27.4	28.0	7.5	35.5
Data security	10.7	24.3	42.9	17.7	4.5	22.2
Digital and video images	23.0	44.0	21.9	7.5	3.6	11.1
Families	4.9	35.7	39.7	16.9	2.8	19.8
Filtering	24.5	43.2	26.7	5.3	0.2	5.6
Governors	5.6	22.9	27.2	33.7	10.6	44.3
Impact of online safety policy and practice	4.4	22.5	30.9	32.5	9.7	42.2
Mobile technology	15.0	47.6	20.5	9.9	7.1	16.9
Monitoring	19.5	45.6	27.4	7.0	0.5	7.5
Online publishing	14.4	39.1	24.6	16.5	5.6	22.1
Online safety education programme	9.9	45.8	30.5	12.3	1.6	13.8
Online safety group	9.0	27.0	19.6	25.4	19.0	44.4
Online safety policy	19.6	53.9	17.4	8.2	1.0	9.2
Online safety responsibilities	17.4	35.5	24.8	21.2	1.1	22.3
Professional standards	22.8	43.4	13.7	14.4	5.7	20.1
Reporting and responding	14.1	32.2	26.7	22.1	4.9	27.0
Social media	11.6	45.8	20.8	14.9	7.0	21.8
Staff	6.6	25.4	35.3	28.3	4.6	32.8
Technical security	14.4	28.9	34.3	19.3	3.1	22.4

they are required to do so, 14% of schools do not have any online safety education programme, and only just over 50% have anything better than basic implementation.

Finally, it is also useful to compare primary and secondary schools to see if there are any differences in practice. This is particularly pertinent when we consider the differences in the ProjectEvolve data below which show how little online safety education is delivered in secondary settings. While the general pattern of the data from primary and secondary schools is similar, there are some differences particularly around those aspects that require technical investment, and some that relate to policy (Table 4.13).

The only aspects where there is a marked (over 0.1) better performance in primary schools is digital and video images, which is reasonable given

Table 4.13   Primary/secondary comparison

	Primary	Secondary	Difference
Acceptable use	2.264	2.173	0.091
Agencies	3.428	3.443	−0.015
Contribution of young people	2.995	3.021	−0.026
Data security	2.855	2.734	0.121
Digital and video images	2.217	2.375	−0.157
Families	2.747	2.813	−0.066
Filtering	2.226	1.887	0.338
Governors	3.196	3.258	−0.062
Impact of online safety policy and practice	3.206	3.249	−0.043
Mobile technology	2.518	2.339	0.179
Monitoring	2.326	1.980	0.346
Online publishing	2.571	2.597	−0.026
Online safety education programme	2.500	2.413	0.087
Online safety group	3.191	3.206	−0.015
Online safety policy	2.149	2.246	−0.097
Online safety responsibilities	2.522	2.561	−0.039
Professional standards	2.391	2.300	0.090
Reporting and responding	2.738	2.658	0.080
Social media	2.628	2.486	0.142
Staff	3.013	2.988	0.025
Technical security	2.772	2.419	0.352

the concerns in primary schools about not sharing images of young children and how this is manage in, for example, school social media.

For secondary schools the better performance around social media policy is equally to be expected, given what is mentioned above but also the perpetual reluctance (in my experience) for primary schools to engage effectively with social media because of the 13-year age limit around the user base.

Where secondary schools also consistently perform higher is with technical aspects, which might be explained because they generally have larger technical resource to invest on managing these aspects (e.g. technical security, filtering and monitoring, and data security). Nevertheless, these are all important aspects for any school setting, data protection duties are no less arduous because a school has a primary setting.

This exploration of the 360 Degree Safe data from England begins to show how the connection between systems within the broader ecosystem might not be as solid as policy makers and regulators might hope to be the case. It begins to show that even where stakeholders (education settings in this case) are regulated, without strong regulatory oversight this might not transfer into practice. This is important because of the growing use of regulation in the ecosystem to mitigate risk and, in the views of policy makers, prevent harms. We will continue this exploration below with an analysis of the ProjectEvolve use in schools.

PROJECTEVOLVE

In 2017 the government, via the UK Council for Internet Safety,[4] established the Education for a Connected World (EfCW). This is a framework developed to support educators in preparing students for life in an increasingly digital world. The framework outlines the knowledge and skills children and young people need to navigate the online environment safely and effectively. The framework is broken down into several different strands:

1. Self-Image and Identity: Exploring how online interactions can affect self-image and identity, and encouraging a positive self-concept.
2. Online Relationships: Understanding how to build and maintain healthy online relationships and recognizing inappropriate or harmful behaviour.
3. Managing Online Information: Learning how to search for information online, evaluate its accuracy, and manage digital footprints.
4. Privacy and Security: Teaching about personal data protection, creating strong passwords, and understanding privacy settings.
5. Copyright and Ownership: Educating about intellectual property, copyright laws, and respecting the creative rights of others.
6. Digital Footprint and Reputation: Understanding how online actions can affect one's digital footprint and long-term reputation.

These aspects were expanded in the 2020 release to also incorporate two further topics:

7. Online Bullying: Understanding bullying and other online aggression and how technology impacts those issues.

---

[4] https://www.gov.uk/government/organisations/uk-council-for-internet-safety [Accessed October 2024]

8. Health, Well-being, and Lifestyle: Exploring the impact that technology has on health, well-being, and lifestyle.

SWGfL developed ProjectEvolve to implement the framework for schools and colleges (therefore tackling one of the key issues in transforming statutory duties into practice). In total, the project implemented 600 age-appropriate resources. These resources are based around eight strands (number of "aspects", or resources, in each strand in parentheses):

- Copyright and Ownership (33);
- Health, Well-being and Lifestyle (40);
- Managing Online Information (73);
- Online Bullying (37);
- Online Relationships (55);
- Online Reputation (30);
- Privacy and Security (58);
- Self Image & Identity (41).

As a fully online system, ProjectEvolve records every interaction with its resource banks and knowledge maps by its users. This, in turn, provides a very detailed picture of the nature of digital literacy education in schools, when and at what level it is delivered, and the knowledge of those making use of the assessment engine. While not explicitly doing so, it also allows us to review the sort of topics that teachers are confident to deliver, and those they do less so.

The following table presents an analysis of data collected within the ProjectEVOLVE database, focusing upon aspects (resources) accessed to help us understand what aspects of online safety education are delivered in schools. This analysis draws upon the data as collected up to May 2024.

The volume of data is such that we can provide a robust analysis of the delivery and assessment of online competencies on a scale impossible to conduct with surveys or case studies. As with the analysis of the 360 Degree Safe data, the volume and quality of this data means we are moving from "we think" we know what goes on in the classroom to "we know" what happens (Table 4.14).

Any school in the country can sign up for an account to use ProjectEVOLVE. Currently, there are over 15,000 schools using it and that number continues to grow—currently well over half of the schools in England use the tool. A school can have more than one "user",

Table 4.14 ProjectEvolve accounts

School accounts	15,221
Users	70,137
Average users per account	4.6
Accounts with more than ten users	2079

Table 4.15 Total ProjectEvolve aspect views

Aspect views	1,177,665
Average number of aspects per user	29.6
Users accessing more than 100	2460
Users accessing more than 500	122

representing the platform being used by multiple staff across the institution—that is, being used by different classroom teachers in the school. As can be seen above, over 70,000 unique users are enrolled on the platform. On average, each account has 4.6 users, meaning that between four and five staff are using the platform. However, a lot of schools use the platform far more, with over 2000 accounts having more than ten users.

If we explore at a very basic level, aspect views, we can see that the platform is used a great deal. This is illustrated further if we look at the aspects (lessons) viewed across the platform (Table 4.15):

We can broadly analogize an aspect to a teaching resource. While this does not specifically mean that the aspect was used to deliver a specific classroom lesson, it gives us a clear indication of the sort of topics teachers are interested in and planning to. As can be seen from the above statistics, there have been a lot of aspects accessed across the platform, in total well over 1,000,000 views. On average, almost thirty aspects have been accessed per account (school). However, some make far greater use of the platform, with almost 2500 schools accessing more than 100 and 122 accessing aspects over 500 times. A more detailed analysis of the sort of aspects access, and by whom, is provided in the following section.

Analysis of Aspect Usage

As discussed above, each aspect in the platform is categorized against a EfCW strand that relates to online safety and wider digital literacy. Below we can see how many times a resource related to a specific strand has been accessed which, in turns, tells us the sort of digital safety/literacy lessons

Table 4.16 Aspect
category count

Online relationships	239,384
Self-image and identity	181,981
Managing online information	143,458
Privacy and security	118,110
Online bullying	116,854
Health, well-being, and lifestyle	97,027
Online reputation	84,385
Copyright and ownership	51,668

that have been delivered in schools. Online Relationships (relating to how to build and maintain healthy online relationships and recognizing inappropriate or harmful behaviour) is by far the most popular strand, and Self-Image and Identity (how online interactions can affect self-image and identity) and Managing Online Information (Learning how to search for information online, evaluate its accuracy, and manage digital footprints) are also widely used. We can see that there is a lot of use across all strands, but these three that relate to personal issues and core digital literacy are far more popular than some others (Table 4.16).

Aspects, being classroom resources, are also categorized against Key Stages, which allows us to examine where at what age range lessons related to online safety and digital competencies are delivered. From the summary below, we can see that there is a very clear focus on deliver in key stages 1 and 2, where far more resources are accessed than in secondary schools (Table 4.17):

We can see that most teaching with ProjectEVOLVE happens in primary schools, with by far the biggest proportion being in Key Stage 2. There is a significant tailing off aspect use in secondary schools. Of course, the data above cannot show use that there is no teaching of online safety and digital competencies in secondary schools, because there are other resources that might being used in those settings. However, it does show very clearly that ProjectEVOLVE is used far more in key stages 1 and 2 with over 90% of delivery happening here. This does, once again, show that while all schools have a statutory duty to deliver "online safety" education, there is evidence here to suggest that far more is delivered in primary settings. Given that the online risks associated with adolescence and young adulthood are very different, and often more complex, than those faced by primary aged children, this is certainly a concern that policy makers should note.

Table 4.17   Key stage
use breakdown

Key stage	Percentage views (%)
1	32.63
2	60.90
3	4.17
4	2.30

Table 4.18   Key stages and aspect categories

	Copyright and ownership (%)	Health, well-being, and lifestyle (%)	Managing online information (%)	Online bullying (%)	Online relationships (%)	Online reputation (%)	Privacy and security (%)	Self-image and identity (%)
1	4.99	7.56	12.25	8.70	29.33	8.79	11.89	16.49
2	4.46	10.64	16.73	13.16	18.24	7.43	11.51	17.83
3	7.63	10.66	9.83	11.79	21.14	8.62	11.14	19.20
4	4.38	9.22	10.44	22.45	16.42	16.67	5.87	14.55

In exploring the focus on aspect used across phases, we can break down strand types in different phases, tabulated below (Table 4.18):

While it is impossible to conduct a like for like comparison, given the difference in volume of delivery in secondary schools compared to primaries, we can proportionally explore the nature of the topics delivered in each key stage and can see that there is some variation, with Online Relationships and Managing Online Relationships coverage reducing across the key stages, whereas Self-image and identity increase slightly. We can also see more about Online reputation being delivered in later key stages, and a slight increase in the consideration of the more technical Copyright and ownership. However, there are only a few percentage points difference in most cases, the pattern of the data remains consistent aside from Online relationships.

Finally, when considering the findings from the analysis of aspect views and how we might interpret these are things the classroom teacher chooses to deliver because they either see it as important or it is a topic with which they are comfortable delivering. Given the focus on Online relationships and Self-image and identity illustrated above, it is no surprise that the "top ten" most viewed aspects all relate to these areas (Table 4.19):

Table 4.19   Most popular aspects

I can give examples of how someone might use technology to communicate with others they don't also know offline and explain why this might be risky. (e.g. email, online gaming, a pen-pal in another school/country).	38,545
I can recognize, online or offline, that anyone can say "no"—"please stop"—" I'll tell"—"I'll ask" to somebody who makes them feel sad, uncomfortable, embarrassed, or upset.	15,864
I can explain how identity online can be copied, modified, or altered.	14,662
I can explain what is meant by the term "identity".	14,271
I can recognize that there may be people online who could make someone feel sad, embarrassed, or upset.	14,187
I can explain how my online identity can be different to my offline identity.	13,129
I can give examples of when I should ask permission to do something online and explain why this is important.	11,412
I can explain how other people may look and act differently online and offline.	11,343
I can identify and critically evaluate online content relating to gender, race, religion, disability, culture, and other groups, and explain why it is important to challenge and reject inappropriate representations online.	10,461
I can describe strategies for safe and fun experiences in a range of online social environments (e.g. livestreaming, gaming platforms).	10,214

Once again, we can see a clear focus here around identity and relationships—eight of these aspects are from the Self-Image and Identity strand and two are from Online Relationships. Given the proportion of delivery that takes place in primary school, we should perhaps not be too surprised by this. It is particularly of note that the aspect that is delivered far more than any other is the very traditional (and outdated) "stranger danger" message. While there are many other aspect views that would suggest in some schools other more progressive education is also delivered, it is interesting to see this significant difference in delivery with this one aspect.

If we consider those that have been accessed the fewest times (Table 4.20):

We can see that these tend to be more technical in nature (six from the Privacy and Security strand, two from Managing Online Information and one from Copyright and Ownership), and cover more complex topics such as disinformation, whistleblowing, and other legal issues. We can also see that a number relate to technical measures an individual can take to manage their privacy. As discussed above when considering the 360 Degree Safe analysis, an individual with good technical knowledge of how to manage their online identities and lives is more likely to be resilient and

Table 4.20 Least popular aspects

I can explain the term "whistleblowing" and evaluate when such action may be appropriate or inappropriate.	56
I can assess how those laws can vary depending on country and can give examples of some of the differences and issues that may raise.	65
I can describe anonymous access services (e.g. TOR, Guerilla Mail, DuckDuckGo) and can give examples of how they may be used in both positive and negative contexts.	72
I can explain the value of regular data backup in system recovery, and can give examples of and demonstrate effective practice in how this might be achieved (e.g. removable media, cloud).	73
I can evaluate whether current measures for preventing and responding to copyright theft are fit for purpose, for example, with current social media use and private profiles.	75
I can analyse online material to identify when this is happening and who might benefit.	76
I can describe how and why individuals, organizations or states may saturate online media with selective information and disinformation to deliberately confuse or divide populations.	81
I can identify and assess when data needs to be transferred securely and can describe strategies to achieve this (e.g. encryption, secure services).	82
I can describe how and where to report a data breach.	84
I can assess and comment on the benefits and effectiveness of these.	84

manage risk more effectively when it comes to threats and online harms. However, we can see very clearly that these are not areas of priority in classrooms in England. Nevertheless, it is encouraging to note that all aspects have been accessed to some degree—there is no learning resource in the ProjectEVOLVE platform that has never been used.

Conclusion

In this chapter, we have delved into the practical implementation of national online safety policies within school settings, primarily through the lens of two significant data sources: the 360 Degree Safe and ProjectEVOLVE platforms. Our analysis has revealed a nuanced picture of how schools interpret and enact their statutory responsibilities around online safety, highlighting both areas of success and concern.

Despite clear statutory guidance from the Department for Education on online safety, the reality within schools shows a mixed adherence to these standards. The 360 Degree Safe data highlights that while some areas of policy and technical measures are well established, aspects requiring long-term resource investment and broader stakeholder engagement, such as staff training and governor awareness, are significantly lacking. This suggests that statutory requirements alone are insufficient to guarantee robust online safety practices in all schools.

Our analysis of the ProjectEVOLVE platform further underscores these findings. The platform's extensive use in primary schools contrasts sharply with its underutilization in secondary settings, raising concerns about the continuity and depth of online safety education as students progress through their schooling. Moreover, the focus on less complex topics like online relationships and self-image over more technical aspects like privacy and security indicates a potential gap in comprehensive digital literacy education.

The data from ProjectEVOLVE also reveals a concerning trend: while students show good knowledge in areas frequently assessed, such as health, well-being, and online bullying, there remains a significant proportion of responses in lower categories, particularly in more complex areas like privacy and security. This inconsistency points to a need for more balanced and thorough coverage of online safety topics across all educational stages.

The evidence suggests that the translation of national online safety policy into effective school practice is inconsistent and often falls short of the intended outcomes. The gap between policy and practice is particularly evident in the variability of training, stakeholder engagement, and the depth of digital literacy education provided. If we are to consider this evidence against the ecosystem model in Chap. 1, there is a suggestion with this data that activity in the macrosystem does not necessarily connect with activity in microsystems that are closer to the child, and therefore more likely to have an impact. While in the macrosystems policy makers, NGOs, the media, and industry might battle to "do more" to protect young people from online harms, young people's consistent calls for better education and more informed adults are far more reliant on the stakeholders closer to them in the ecosystem. And the data presented in this chapter highlights that poor training and community engagement, and a tailing off of education around online safety, do little to strengthen the ecosystem at this level.

In the next chapter, we will consider the central point in the ecosystem—young people themselves and explore what they have told us about their needs to address online harms and, in doing so, considers the impact of policy positions on their needs.

References

Department for Education. (2023). *Keeping children safe in education.* Accessed October 2024, from https://assets.publishing.service.gov.uk/media/64f0a68ea78c5f000dc6f3b2/Keeping_children_safe_in_education_2023.pdf

OFSTED. (2024). *School inspection handbook.* Accessed October 2024, from https://www.gov.uk/government/publications/school-inspection-handbook-eif/school-inspection-handbook-for-september-2023

CHAPTER 5

The Silent Youth Voice

Abstract This chapter highlights the gap between policy makers' perspectives and young people's actual concerns about online harms. Based on a survey of over 16,000 young people, the chapter reveals that youths primarily worry about peer conflict, social media pressures, and distressing current events, rather than the extreme content that often dominates policy discussions. The findings suggest that while policy makers advocate for restrictive measures against platforms, young people place more value on knowledgeable, supportive adults who understand the digital issues they face. The chapter also discusses the erosion of trust in adults, especially educators, who are often perceived as poorly informed, leading many young people to rely on peers for support. These insights underscore the need for a youth-centred approach in online safety, emphasizing effective education, empathetic adult involvement, and support that aligns more closely with young people's lived experiences.

Keywords Youth voice • Peer conflict • Policy disconnect • Trust erosion • Youth-centric policy

In developing the theme of tension between the grassroots and policy direction, this chapter explores the main missing stakeholder perspective in these debates—input from young people themselves. While there are

A. Phippen, *Policy and Rights Challenges in Children's Online Behaviour and Safety, 2017–2023*,
https://doi.org/10.1007/978-3-031-80286-7_5

many in the policy space who claim to represent young people, the reality is that what is discussed on parliamentary estate is very different from authentic youth voice. Drawing upon quantitative data from a survey of over 16,000 young people conducted over the last five years, we highlight conflict in a number of areas:

- Young people's views on harmful content and online harms are not what is discussed by policy makers.
- They are far more likely to voice concern on what might be viewed as more mundane, such as peer on peer conflict, social media anxiety, and the impact of current affairs, than concerns around more "extreme" content, such as pornography, terrorism, and self-harm, all of which are disclosed and discussed far less.
- Due to a lack of knowledge by adults with safeguarding responsibilities, and poor educational messages, they are far more likely to turn to peers for help which can result in problematic outcomes
- Frustrations with adult support—which they view as education generally poorly delivered by staff who do not understand the issues in depth, or challenging conversations with parents informed not by evidence but the latest moral panic instigated by the media.
- Perhaps most significantly, for a policy direction that expects "the solution" to be all risk mitigation being tackled through the platforms themselves, there is a great deal of mistrust in reporting tools and platform response.

This data is presented as part of the proposition that what is going on in the policy space does not reflect the needs of young people. We discussed in the early chapters of this book that while there had been an acceleration in policy over the last twenty years, what young people called for in discussions with them has not changed. This large dataset allows us to articulate this very clearly and be in no doubt of the gulf between what young people and what policy makers decide is best for them.

A Large Survey of Young People's Views on the Use of Digital Technology and Online Harms

Another part of my long-term work with SWGfL is a survey with schools with whom the charity works. The survey is disseminated to schools prior to visits by consultants who are commissioned to do work with them (either in the classroom or training with staff and parents). Schools run the survey in class so a broad cross-section of respondents is reached, and we have some control of the validity of responses that would not be achieved through anonymous dissemination. Since commencement of the latest version of the survey in February 2016 we have collected data from 16,359 responses, and it is from these responses that we present this analysis. I am mindful that there is a lot of numerical data presented here, which can be a little overwhelming. However, it is a very useful breakdown regarding what a lot of young people tell us about their online lives and the concerns they have around online harms. Given the size of the respondent population, we can be confident that this is reliable dataset that gives us a true picture. And given that it is administered in schools, in class, we are equally confident that this is a strong cross-section of all young people.

The survey was constructed to collect basic information on:

- online usage (devices, kinds of activity, time online),
- upsetting content (both frequency and type of upset),
- issues related to abuse (saying or receiving abusive comments),
- the sorts of things that cause upset online,
- views related to online safety and well-being, and
- controls of their internet use.

The current version of the survey can be seen at: https://www.survey-monkey.co.uk/r/ypinternet

The survey is a useful tool for exploring policy around online safeguarding because it is a large database of young people's views on these issues and, due to be collected over a long period, we are confident that these views are representative and present a consistent picture of young people's views. Below we present data drawn from the top level of the survey to look at total responses, but also broken down in terms of gender and age to show how behaviour and need adapts as young people get older. Towards the end of the chapter, we will also look at two other areas of focus—differences in the application of "house rules" to show the impact of parental engagement, and a comparison of responses five years apart, to show areas of change.

Of those respondents, 48% were male and 50.5% female; 1% did not disclose gender and 0.5% self-described.

The age range collected for the survey is broad from year 4 (aged 8–9) to year 13 (aged 17–18). There is around a 50/50 split between those in primary education and those at secondary school, however, as we can see from the table below, the focus is around what we would refer to in England as "key stages 2 and 3", so between the ages of 8 and 13. There are parallels here with the ProjectEvolve data, which shows the drop off in engagement with online safety practice through secondary school (Table 5.1).

When asking about how young people access digital services and platforms, it is a little surprising that the predominant device for going online is the mobile phone. We can also see when we look at the school year breakdown that there is a marked increase in mobile phone use in year 7 (when young people transition to secondary school). However, we can also see that many younger children also access online services using a mobile (Ofcom, 2024). Similarly, younger children might access online services via a tablet, but this use will drop as they get older (and most likely gain a mobile phone) (Table 5.2).

This data, of itself, tells us little about online risk or young people's concerns; however, it does show that young people are likely to access online services via a variety of devices from a young age.

In terms of screen time (asked "How much time do you spend online in an average day?"), again we can see that there are differences in

Table 5.1 Year group breakdown

Year	%	
Year 2	8.52%	1394
Year 3	3.98%	651
Year 4	4.52%	740
Year 5	14.08%	2304
Year 6	17.08%	2794
Year 7	11.82%	1933
Year 8	10.93%	1788
Year 9	9.74%	1594
Year 10	7.43%	1215
Year 11	6.00%	981
Year 12	3.26%	533
Year 13	2.64%	432

Table 5.2 Device use

	Mobile (%)	Laptop (%)	Tablet (%)	Home gaming (%)	Mobile gaming (%)	Desktop pc (%)	Television (%)
Overall	75.85	57.75	57.44	43.83	17.25	27.20	50.13
Male	73.56	54.39	56.00	63.79	23.94	33.00	51.70
Female	78.30	61.22	59.33	24.94	11.39	21.72	48.92
Year 3	41.15	42.42	64.59	31.58	19.46	19.14	49.92
Year 4	44.12	47.03	68.05	38.73	24.76	18.40	53.80
Year 5	56.08	48.06	70.40	48.50	24.58	25.46	55.29
Year 6	72.61	50.29	66.01	52.41	22.57	26.99	55.51
Year 7	88.28	57.48	55.86	44.45	14.54	27.88	47.42
Year 8	90.70	59.30	57.01	42.71	13.68	29.99	51.57
Year 9	94.03	67.92	43.02	43.52	11.07	30.06	46.42
Year 10	94.64	71.06	41.14	43.20	11.05	30.92	46.50
Year 11	97.34	74.69	42.42	38.83	9.22	30.53	45.08
Year 12	97.36	81.54	35.40	29.94	5.65	27.12	40.11
Year 13	96.50	88.55	35.75	29.67	6.07	29.67	36.68

different age groups, typically the older a young person is, the more time they spend online. While this might be due to greater social interactions online, it is equally likely to be related to the increase in the use of digital technology for schoolwork. Again, as discussed already in this book, there is little causal link between screen time and negative impacts upon the child, there are over 10% of year 3 (aged 7–8) young people online for more than six hours a day (Table 5.3).

Finally, in terms of "scene-setting" questions, we also ask respondents what they do online. These are broad ranging categories that let us gain insight into the types of activities young people do online. Listening to music is the most popular, by a few percentage points, but it is interesting to note the split in percentages between male and female respondents related to gaming, which is a far more popular activity among males. Nevertheless, while it might traditionally be viewed as a male pastime, over half of our female respondents said that play video games online. It is also interesting to note that while social media use among very young children is low, there is a significant increase in year 5/6, between the ages of 9 and 11. By the time young people reach the traditional "age 13 restriction" on social media, in year 8, most young people are already using it. As already discussed, this somewhat arbitrary and data protection-oriented age barrier has become something of an excuse for not delivering education around social media (we came across many professionals in the Headstart

Table 5.3   Screen time

	Less than an hour (%)	One to three hours (%)	Between 3 and 6 hours (%)	More than 6 hours (%)
Overall	20.74	41.58	25.84	11.84
Male	18.37	42.07	26.24	13.31
Female	22.86	41.54	25.39	10.21
Year 3	41.98	35.17	12.80	10.05
Year 4	36.50	41.40	14.41	7.69
Year 5	32.58	42.93	16.00	8.49
Year 6	23.96	46.04	21.54	8.46
Year 7	20.38	48.34	22.12	9.16
Year 8	12.33	46.27	30.20	11.20
Year 9	6.63	42.89	33.92	16.55
Year 10	5.38	36.42	42.05	16.14
Year 11	3.59	33.13	44.00	19.28
Year 12	3.21	27.74	46.23	22.83
Year 13	1.85	29.63	42.59	25.93

project that said social media should not be covered in primary schools because "they shouldn't be on it" and many beliefs that the age limit exists for safeguarding reasons) conflicts with the reality in a lot of "under-aged" young people using these services.

Similarly, we can also see an increase in the use of messaging platforms (also generally bound by the 13 age limit) towards the end of primary school which, while legal problematic (for platforms who might be held liable for data collected by these under aged users) highlights how important it is to start education around empathetic and responsible messaging at an earlier age that is often the case (Table 5.4).

We now consider results from questions that relate to upset online, and this is where we will examine the data in more depth and this is particularly important when considering the main goal in this book, which is to explore the gulf between stakeholders and young people when considering online harms and how to support young people. We start with a basic question about whether they have ever seen anything online that has upset them. As we can see, most young people have not, with just under a third of young people saying they have. Female respondents are more likely to say that they have seen something upsetting online, and unexpectedly, as young people get older, they are more likely, being more engaged and having more mature online interactions, to have been upset by something (Table 5.5).

Table 5.4   Online activity

	Social networks (%)	Messaging (%)	Gaming (%)	Shopping (%)	News (%)	Browsing (%)	Music (%)	Content creation (%)
Overall	51.05	43.33	68.97	36.73	24.32	49.21	71.63	24.51
Male	46.73	39.35	86.28	30.33	27.29	49.70	66.07	28.30
Female	55.58	47.05	51.85	43.17	21.65	49.32	77.00	21.04
Year 3	10.77	13.05	79.45	16.31	18.27	18.43	45.19	28.06
Year 4	11.72	17.43	85.22	17.43	14.78	24.83	56.07	23.43
Year 5	24.54	31.45	81.47	21.53	17.00	36.52	63.48	31.81
Year 6	37.65	44.91	78.98	25.85	18.77	45.10	68.73	31.19
Year 7	54.44	51.48	64.41	35.43	19.38	51.95	73.44	24.97
Year 8	71.09	55.78	60.66	46.37	25.00	60.09	79.54	21.37
Year 9	79.86	53.18	58.70	49.87	25.98	62.90	81.45	19.63
Year 10	83.72	54.32	57.56	54.57	35.13	69.85	84.30	16.11
Year 11	89.46	55.89	50.56	63.66	41.76	68.99	88.13	15.46
Year 12	90.94	57.36	49.06	66.79	50.57	75.09	86.98	12.08
Year 13	90.26	58.24	41.30	69.84	58.24	77.03	87.47	12.53

Table 5.5   Online upset

Have you ever seen anything online that has made you feel upset?

	Yes (%)	No (%)
Overall	32.96	67.04
Male	28.08	71.92
Female	36.91	63.09
Year 3	28.57	71.43
Year 4	26.93	73.07
Year 5	27.16	72.84
Year 6	30.47	69.53
Year 7	26.28	73.72
Year 8	32.79	67.21
Year 9	37.47	62.53
Year 10	40.18	59.82
Year 11	47.49	52.51
Year 12	49.43	50.57
Year 13	49.07	50.93

Table 5.6 What causes upset

What causes upset? (top 25 words)

People	511	YouTube	86
Someone	307	Abuse	78
Upset	177	Anything	68
Video	161	Messages	66
Online	149	Stuff	56
Videos	148	Nasty	56
Bullying	120	Swearing	54
Comments	119	Upsetting	53
Rude	113	Racism	52
Mean	110	Roblox	51
Game	104	Racist	50
Something	100	Momo	50
Scary	89		

In the first instance, this might suggest a justification for prohibitive legislation that prevents young people from seeing the subjectively defined "harmful" content. However, the follow-up question to this asked the respondent to describe what causes them to be upset, and we list the top twenty-five words that come from these free text responses below (Table 5.6):

And if we use a word cloud to see what causes upset, we see a response that aligns more with the findings of the discussions with young people as part of the Headstart project (Fig. 5.1):

Simply put, young people tell us that the main cause of upset online is "people", and this has been the case over the duration of the survey (see Phippen, 2017 for an analysis on an earlier dataset). If we explore the types of disclosures we received, we can see a mix of person-to-person abuse and some forms of content. However, the content express does not necessarily align with the goals of the Online Safety Act 2023 and other forms of online safety legislation. The key themes coming from these disclosures are:

- Animal Abuse: Many respondents mentioned videos or images of animals being mistreated or killed as particularly upsetting. For example, seeing a video of a dog being abused, a cat being put in a blender, or a dog waiting for its owner who never comes were frequently cited as distressing.

Fig. 5.1 What causes upset online?

- Peer on Peer Abuse: Numerous individuals described experiences of being called names, receiving threats, or witnessing others being bullied online. For instance, one person mentioned being called a "cry baby" after sharing that they had a nightmare from watching a scary video. There were further examples such as being called a "noob" and receiving mean comments on gaming platforms like Roblox. And other instances included someone being bullied by their friends and feeling left out or targeted in group chats.
- Current Affairs: A significant number of respondents talk about being upset by things that relate to current affairs and news broadcasts. Respondents have referred in a timely way to significant world events such as the climate crisis, the Ukraine war, the Israel/Gaza conflict, and terrorist incidents.
- Scary Content: Content young people described as "scary" in videos, images, or story form were frequently mentioned. For example, the "Momo"challenge was mentioned multiple times and this relates directly back to the impact of moral panics explored in Chap. 3. As another means of assessing the impact of adult-initiated moral panics, we can see mention of Momo before and after "Momo week" (Table 5.7):

Table 5.7 Mentions of Momo in disclosures

Responses before February 24, 2019 (*n* = 8778):	2931
Mentions of Momo by respondents before February 24, 2019:	0
Responses since March 1, 2019: (*n* = 7436)	2215
Mentions of Momo by respondents since March 1, 2019:	50

- Death and Illness: Content about death and terminal illness was a significant source of distress. For example, stories about children or beloved pets dying, or watching a sad movie about someone with cancer, were frequently mentioned. One respondent was upset by seeing a video of a child who had cancer and eventually died.
- Sad Stories and Movies: Movies and stories with sad themes caused emotional distress for some respondents. For instance, respondents mentioned being upset by sad TikTok videos about people with cancer or seeing a dog dying in a sad song. Another example includes watching a movie at a sleepover that was rated 18+ and feeling uncomfortable and distressed by the content.
- Racism and Discrimination: Instances of racism, homophobia, and other forms of discrimination were significant sources of distress. For example, one respondent mentioned seeing racist comments about their religion while another mentioned being upset by homophobic content online. Another example was a young person feeling distressed by comments that were racist or discriminatory towards minority groups they had seen in group chats.

These examples illustrate the wide range of upsetting content and experiences described in the document, reflecting both personal and broader societal concerns. Therefore, if we start to unpick this from a prohibitive legislative perspective, if we are aiming to prevent young people from being exposed to anything harmful online, we can see how complex and, arguably, impossible, this will be. Unless we are proposing that young people should be removed from all social and mainstream media platforms, given that a lot of disclosures related to current affairs and conventional entertainment such as movies, a prohibitive approach, based upon this data, would have significant impact upon young people's human rights. Clearly, as explored in Chap. 1, there are some who would propose such a ban. However, it is not realistic to expect young people to be shielded for all forms of online interaction and mainstream media until an arbitrary age, given some have disclosed upset as a result.

In exploring their own behaviour online, we also asked whether they had ever said anything nasty to someone online, and whether they had received nasty comments. Unsurprisingly, fewer young people said they had said something nasty that they had received upsetting comments. Across all years there is a significant minority who have said nasty comments to someone online, and there is a slight gender difference. However, we should caveat this with the fact that, as discussed above, some young people have said they do not appreciate what online abuse is, so there is a chance some might have been abusive without recognizing it as such. For example, many gamers disclose using offensive language to other players but see this as part of the gaming experience rather than something abusive (Table 5.8).

It is interesting to note that even in the receiving on comments, all except year 11 responses have the majority saying they have not. Which reflects a different picture to media narratives that portray the "dangers" of young people being online. While there are clearly lots of disclosures in these responses that are cause for concern and highlight the need to provide supporting environments for young people wishing to get support

Table 5.8 Saying online abuse

Have you ever said anything nasty to someone online?

	Yes (%)	*No (%)*
Overall	15.67	84.33
Male	19.92	80.08
Female	11.34	88.66
Year 3	6.75	93.25
Year 4	7.54	92.46
Year 5	10.44	89.56
Year 6	12.79	87.21
Year 7	12.44	87.56
Year 8	16.82	83.18
Year 9	24.13	75.87
Year 10	23.43	76.57
Year 11	30.11	69.89
Year 12	28.46	71.54
Year 13	24.42	75.58

regarding online incidents, it also shows that most of the time, most young people are having positive experiences online. However, that is not a particularly click bait media headline or a message for a funding chasing charity to put out (Table 5.9).

In another part of the survey, we run a group of five-point Likert scale tests against a number of statements to measure young people's attitudes to online issues. The first one was included because of the popular trope that "Young people know more than their parents about online issues". As we can see, this is not necessarily the case and while most young people who do believe this grows as they get older, there are still many who do not (Table 5.10).

A more telling test is asking whether they feel what they do online is of no concern of their parents. With the responses to this question, it is clear that young people very much disagree with this, and do not wish to hide their online lives from their parents. And while the proportion who agree with the statement increases as they get older, they are still in the minority in all cases (Table 5.11).

There were also several statements to consider well-being related issues. In the first the statement that they think they spend too much time online is asked. For the next four statements the comparison is also made with screen time, given the purported links between screen time and well-being.

Table 5.9 Receiving online abuse

Have you ever received nasty comments/content online?

	Yes (%)	No (%)
Overall	35.98	64.02
Male	38.53	61.47
Female	33.01	66.99
Year 3	19.62	80.38
Year 4	22.63	77.37
Year 5	28.66	71.34
Year 6	36.30	63.70
Year 7	34.03	65.97
Year 8	37.87	62.13
Year 9	45.61	54.39
Year 10	45.91	54.09
Year 11	52.66	47.34
Year 12	49.53	50.47
Year 13	49.77	50.23

Table 5.10 I know more about the internet than my parents

I know more about the internet than my parents

	Strongly agree (%)	Agree (%)	No opinion (%)	Disagree (%)	Strongly disagree (%)
Overall	25.20	27.78	19.45	17.44	10.14
Male	29.21	25.17	18.76	17.00	9.86
Female	21.02	30.41	20.14	18.03	10.41
Year 3	12.86	11.59	16.67	32.86	26.03
Year 4	9.86	15.07	23.56	30.41	21.10
Year 5	17.51	20.36	23.42	22.89	15.82
Year 6	17.61	26.29	24.01	21.52	10.56
Year 7	19.65	30.87	24.27	18.40	6.81
Year 8	27.43	34.23	20.85	12.59	4.89
Year 9	33.46	37.32	17.27	8.98	2.97
Year 10	40.61	36.08	14.66	6.59	2.06
Year 11	49.85	35.04	8.48	4.39	2.25
Year 12	47.18	38.35	6.95	6.20	1.32
Year 13	54.52	31.55	6.26	5.10	2.55

Table 5.11 It is none of my parents' business what I do online

It is none of my parents' business what I do online

	Strongly agree (%)	Agree (%)	No opinion (%)	Disagree (%)	Strongly disagree (%)
Overall	7.75	13.53	23.16	31.35	24.22
Male	10.12	14.21	22.60	29.32	23.75
Female	5.31	12.69	23.40	33.66	24.94
Year 3	11.27	9.64	12.25	24.35	42.48
Year 4	6.63	7.46	14.92	29.56	41.44
Year 5	7.24	8.27	14.30	29.54	40.66
Year 6	4.89	8.99	18.41	35.04	32.68
Year 7	3.65	9.70	23.94	39.59	23.11
Year 8	7.48	12.87	29.57	36.99	13.10
Year 9	7.46	17.46	35.29	31.56	8.22
Year 10	9.14	21.66	34.18	28.75	6.26
Year 11	13.32	27.66	34.02	21.82	3.18
Year 12	9.62	35.85	28.49	23.77	2.26
Year 13	16.47	31.09	25.29	23.67	3.48

Certainly, there are many young people who are concerned about the time they spend online which, given they are in control (to a certain extent) with how much time they spend online is a curious response. However, as we have already discussed as they get older there is a great need to do schoolwork online, and the fear of missing out looms here too. It is interesting to note that those who spend a long of time online are more likely to be concerned, but there is a subsection of this group that are less concerned than those who spend less time online. It is also interesting to note that even 15% of those who spend less than an hour a day online worry that it is too much (Table 5.12).

Thankfully the statement "I worry about things I've seen online" shows a significant majority not worried, which again contrasts with the perceived wisdom about how distressing the online world is for young people. Those that are worried about things they see tend to be younger, and those who spend more time online (Table 5.13).

Table 5.12 I think I spend too much time online

I think I spend too much time online

	Strongly agree (%)	Agree (%)	No opinion (%)	Disagree (%)	Strongly disagree (%)
Overall	10.98	24.99	26.09	24.30	13.64
Male	10.48	22.11	27.09	24.66	15.67
Female	11.31	27.98	25.05	24.24	11.42
Year 3	13.79	17.90	20.69	19.70	27.91
Year 4	11.60	18.65	27.90	23.34	18.51
Year 5	10.62	19.27	22.21	27.03	20.87
Year 6	9.98	19.81	27.60	27.39	15.22
Year 7	8.19	25.23	30.34	25.44	10.79
Year 8	9.40	26.30	32.15	24.61	7.55
Year 9	11.14	28.99	27.47	23.80	8.61
Year 10	9.74	33.20	27.33	23.29	6.44
Year 11	14.08	37.10	25.08	17.37	6.37
Year 12	15.04	40.60	22.18	19.74	2.44
Year 13	17.95	40.79	19.35	17.48	4.43
< 1 hour	3.45	12.20	19.29	38.58	26.48
1–3 hours	6.21	26.85	29.30	28.23	9.41
3–6 hours	17.55	32.98	25.59	14.33	9.55
> 6 hours	27.87	20.72	17.68	12.15	21.58

Table 5.13 I worry about things I have seen online

I worry about things I have seen online

	Strongly agree (%)	Agree (%)	No opinion (%)	Disagree (%)	Strongly disagree (%)
Overall	6.47	15.22	23.40	29.11	25.79
Male	5.90	13.17	21.54	28.78	30.62
Female	6.76	17.05	25.06	29.80	21.32
Year 3	14.53	16.05	19.93	20.44	29.05
Year 4	12.32	16.71	19.97	25.50	25.50
Year 5	8.55	14.80	21.70	24.05	30.90
Year 6	5.70	13.81	19.89	28.03	32.57
Year 7	4.26	12.89	24.77	31.43	26.64
Year 8	2.80	13.39	27.70	32.63	23.47
Year 9	5.28	14.23	26.34	32.52	21.64
Year 10	4.11	15.79	24.69	37.95	17.46
Year 11	5.49	18.34	29.64	31.61	14.92
Year 12	3.02	23.77	23.02	36.79	13.40
Year 13	4.22	20.61	26.00	31.15	18.03
< 1 hour	5.16	13.78	21.38	27.18	32.49
1–3 hours	5.15	14.60	21.90	31.60	26.75
3–6 hours	7.58	15.21	24.55	29.24	23.41
> 6 hours	11.22	14.11	24.11	22.44	28.11

There are similar responses to the statement regarding being unable to sleep because of things that happen online, with it only applying to the minority, and those who are concerned tend to be younger. And again those who spend a lot of time online are slightly more likely to agree with the statement (Table 5.14).

Finally, loneliness is a statement where there is, again, a majority who disagree but in this case, there is a large minority who agree with the statement. This is most clear with those who spend a lot of time online, and those who are older. Certainly, this is a most clear differentiation between statement response and time spent online (Table 5.15).

The final part of the survey explores what rules there are at home regarding going online and who they would disclose to if they were concerned about something. The first question simply asks whether there are rules at home, and we can see that in most cases there are. This is slightly more likely for female respondents, and with those who are younger. As

Table 5.14   I sometimes can't sleep because I am thinking about things that happened online

I sometimes can't sleep because I am thinking about things that happened online				
	Strongly agree (%)	*Agree (%)*	*No opinion (%)*	*Disagree (%)*	*Strongly disagree (%)*
Overall	5.92	11.08	14.21	24.54	44.25
Male	5.85	9.21	12.94	22.60	49.40
Female	5.81	12.80	15.35	26.44	39.60
Year 3	15.95	13.79	13.79	19.44	37.04
Year 4	11.99	16.74	12.27	23.85	35.15
Year 5	7.67	12.65	13.86	18.88	46.95
Year 6	5.95	10.77	12.97	22.13	48.17
Year 7	3.40	8.62	15.41	27.38	45.19
Year 8	3.11	9.89	13.85	28.55	44.60
Year 9	3.99	10.51	15.71	27.42	42.37
Year 10	3.39	9.26	15.12	28.18	44.05
Year 11	3.50	12.24	15.74	29.22	39.30
Year 12	2.27	9.85	11.93	34.47	41.48
Year 13	2.56	6.05	14.88	25.58	50.93
< 1 hour	3.76	8.89	13.50	23.01	50.83
1–3 hours	4.44	10.09	13.17	23.51	48.78
3–6 hours	5.86	11.87	15.06	24.81	42.40
> 6 hours	10.99	11.64	14.25	20.24	42.87

we might expect, as the age range increases, the number of respondents who still have house rules decreases (Table 5.16).

When asked what sort of rules there are, it is equally unsurprising that the main rules relate to time limits and times of day that young people cannot go online. However, there is also many respondents whose parents can look at what they are doing online. While this is, as expected, prevalent with younger children, over 20% of respondents still say that is the case when they are well into their teens (Table 5.17).

However, we can also see that the majority of respondents have ways to get around these restrictions, and this increases as they get older. This reiterates the issue that rules can be useful to set boundaries, but young people will find work around so should not be viewed as guarantees of ways to reduce online harms. There is a balance to be had between parental support and encroachment onto young people's rights (Table 5.18).

Table 5.15 I go online when I am lonely

I go online when I am lonely

	Strongly agree (%)	Agree (%)	No opinion (%)	Disagree (%)	Strongly disagree (%)
Overall	12.38	21.02	23.79	20.88	21.94
Male	12.87	18.65	23.18	21.14	24.16
Female	11.60	23.10	24.17	20.89	20.24
Year 3	14.85	17.16	20.63	18.48	28.88
Year 4	14.79	18.87	21.83	20.70	23.80
Year 5	12.76	19.02	22.39	18.96	26.88
Year 6	12.64	18.56	24.43	20.43	23.94
Year 7	10.13	18.07	24.38	23.62	23.80
Year 8	10.13	22.19	25.87	20.19	21.63
Year 9	12.60	20.95	24.70	22.83	18.93
Year 10	9.98	22.87	26.79	22.53	17.83
Year 11	13.17	26.45	23.16	22.28	14.93
Year 12	11.17	33.71	25.19	20.83	9.09
Year 13	10.53	31.58	22.25	20.81	14.83
< 1 hour	5.63	13.94	22.68	25.49	32.25
1–3 hours	9.10	20.80	24.21	22.11	23.78
3–6 hours	14.03	24.69	24.50	16.68	20.10
> 6 hours	25.61	17.39	20.35	14.29	22.37

Table 5.16 Rules at home

Are there any rules at home for using the internet?

	Yes (%)	No (%)
Overall	66.53	33.47
Male	64.94	35.06
Female	67.83	32.17
Year 3	72.37	27.63
Year 4	82.46	17.54
Year 5	80.09	19.91
Year 6	78.32	21.68
Year 7	75.08	24.92
Year 8	66.33	33.67
Year 9	57.74	42.26
Year 10	50.46	49.54
Year 11	35.25	64.75
Year 12	23.92	76.08
Year 13	20.84	79.16

Table 5.17   Types of home rules

If yes, what sort of rules are there (please tick all that apply)?

	Parents control access to sites I can visit (%)	Ages restrictions on internet access (%)	Parents can see what I look at online (%)	Only allowed online for a certain amount of time (%)	Not allowed online after a certain time in the evening (%)	Only allowed to go online in family rooms, e.g. living room/ kitchen (%)
Overall	38.75	38.30	46.18	50.51	51.83	14.91
Male	36.70	36.99	43.80	51.19	50.81	14.79
Female	40.96	39.43	48.41	49.83	52.53	14.94
Year 3	42.63	30.51	54.75	58.18	42.42	22.83
Year 4	49.24	41.01	53.28	62.35	48.07	22.02
Year 5	42.35	40.92	54.62	55.94	50.29	16.61
Year 6	39.45	40.51	51.32	51.55	49.98	13.06
Year 7	38.46	43.30	47.62	50.04	53.55	12.45
Year 8	35.94	41.10	37.54	46.98	57.47	12.01
Year 9	32.61	37.06	32.27	39.34	58.38	10.83
Year 10	27.72	31.80	26.19	40.48	55.61	10.88
Year 11	26.71	27.00	22.85	40.36	59.35	10.09
Year 12	28.00	32.80	21.60	29.60	52.80	11.20
Year 13	27.50	35.00	21.25	33.75	48.75	7.50

Table 5.18   Getting around home rules

If you answered yes to rules at home, do you know how to get around these restrictions?

	Yes (%)	No (%)	Some of them (%)
Overall	27.00	39.18	33.82
Male	28.53	38.82	32.65
Female	25.03	39.57	35.40
Year 3	25.72	36.41	37.86
Year 4	22.46	40.42	37.13
Year 5	25.54	37.25	37.20
Year 6	25.91	38.80	35.28
Year 7	23.03	41.39	35.57
Year 8	24.44	42.54	33.02
Year 9	30.57	40.12	29.31
Year 10	33.57	37.22	29.21
Year 11	41.71	36.02	22.27
Year 12	44.00	32.00	24.00
Year 13	36.80	43.20	20.00

Finally, we can see from the last question who young people are most likely to turn to if they are concerned about something upsetting online. It reiterates the importance of the parent as a key stakeholder in young people's safety online, as this is the most likely stakeholder they will turn to. We can see that this reduces as they get older, and asking friends for support increases, but at no point are young people who would not turn to their parents for help in the minority. Perhaps most concerning, given the amount of time spend in schools, is the low number of young people who would ask a teacher for help. While there is a reasonable (but not majority) level in primary settings, there is a significant minority in secondary schools. We also provided an "other" category for this question, which elicited both inciteful and amusing responses. However, one of the most telling things to come from this was that there was not a single response that said they would make use of the platform's reporting to address an issue. Which is highly indicative of the gulf between some stakeholders who believe that platforms should prevent any harms occurring on their platforms, and young people who do not consider the platform someone who could help. This is something we will return to in a later chapter, but it is a clear illustration of the gulf in attitudes between young people and their safeguarding stakeholders (Table 5.19).

Table 5.19 Getting support

Who would you turn to if you were upset by something that happened online (please tick all that apply)?

	Friends (%)	Parents (%)	Other family member (%)	School/teacher (%)	Police (%)
Overall	59.91	82.74	39.83	30.41	16.45
Male	54.68	83.81	40.98	29.92	19.46
Female	64.85	82.08	38.65	31.01	13.46
Year 3	41.96	87.78	46.95	40.19	18.65
Year 4	43.38	90.28	45.77	39.15	12.11
Year 5	47.41	91.46	50.36	38.60	19.57
Year 6	51.27	91.52	48.65	37.93	19.39
Year 7	60.49	87.73	42.43	33.19	16.16
Year 8	69.21	81.11	34.81	22.20	13.56
Year 9	72.22	75.12	28.52	18.81	14.03
Year 10	76.76	66.79	26.09	17.63	10.86
Year 11	81.56	60.52	23.42	15.84	11.76
Year 12	84.38	63.89	18.26	16.02	13.79
Year 13	86.58	59.21	20.79	15.00	14.21

In bringing this exploration of the survey data to a close, there are two subsets of respondents that will be explored further. Firstly, given the importance of the parental stakeholder in disclosure, it is interesting to explore the differences between those who have house rules and those who do not, given this is a useful indicator of parental interest in a young person's online interactions. While this will not be a question-by-question examination, it is useful to see where there are clear differences.

Firstly, those without house rules are more likely to have a mobile phone to go online, and more likely to have a laptop (Table 5.20).

And they are more likely to spend more time online, in significant amounts, than those who have rules at home (Table 5.21):

We can see that they are also more likely to be on social media, and engage in online shopping if there are no house rules (Table 5.22).

And significantly more likely to both say nasty things to others online, and also receive upsetting comments (Tables 5.23 and 5.24).

In terms of attitudinal statements, those without house rules are far more likely to believe what they do online is none of their parents' business, and they also know more about the online world than their parents do (Tables 5.25 and 5.26).

Table 5.20 No house rules device use

What do you use to go online? (please tick all you use)

	Mobile/ smart phone (%)	Laptop (%)	Tablet (%)	Home gaming devices (%)	Mobile gaming devices (%)	PC (%)	Television (%)
Yes	71.70	55.62	60.81	43.26	17.58	27.02	51.84
No	84.51	62.13	50.29	45.03	16.34	27.53	46.96
Diff	12.81	6.51	−10.51	1.77	−1.24	0.51	−4.88

Table 5.21 No house rules screen time

How much time do you spend online in an average day?

	Less than an hour (%)	One to three hours (%)	Between 3 and 6 hours (%)	More than 6 hours (%)
Yes	25.50	45.96	21.28	7.26
No	10.99	33.17	35.07	20.77
Difference	−14.51	−12.79	13.79	13.51

Table 5.22   No house rules types of activity

What do you use the internet for?

	Social networks (%)	Instant messaging (%)	Gaming (%)	Shopping (%)	News (%)	Browsing/general entertainment (%)	Listening to music (%)	Uploading content creation (%)
Yes	43.46	40.67	71.61	31.34	22.55	46.74	70.13	24.85
No	66.24	48.96	63.53	47.58	27.72	54.68	75.09	23.64
Difference	22.78	8.29	−8.08	16.24	5.17	7.94	4.96	−1.21

Table 5.23 No house rules saying online abuse

Have you ever said anything nasty to someone online?

	Yes (%)	*No (%)*
Yes	12.28	87.72
No	22.31	77.69
Difference	10.03	−10.03

Table 5.24 No house rules receiving online abuse

Have you ever received nasty comments/content online?

	Yes (%)	*No (%)*
Yes	33.54	66.46
No	40.94	59.06
Difference	7.40	−7.40

Table 5.25 No house rules "I know more about the internet than my parents"

I know more about the internet than my parents

	Strongly agree (%)	*Agree (%)*	*No opinion (%)*	*Disagree (%)*	*Strongly disagree (%)*
Yes	19.13	26.54	21.44	21.08	11.81
No	37.23	30.45	15.45	10.07	6.81
Difference	18.10	3.91	−5.99	−11.01	−5.00

Table 5.26 No house rules "It is none of my parents' business what I do online"

It is none of my parents' business what I do online

	Strongly agree (%)	*Agree (%)*	*No opinion (%)*	*Disagree (%)*	*Strongly disagree (%)*
Yes	5.72	9.86	19.39	34.56	30.47
No	11.64	20.64	30.62	25.27	11.83
Difference	5.92	10.78	11.23	−9.29	−18.64

And there is a slightly higher likelihood that will feel they spend too much time online (Table 5.27).

Perhaps most telling, however, is that this group of respondents are far less likely, across many adult stakeholders, to turn to them for support, and are far more likely to ask friends for help (Table 5.28).

While, clearly, there is no means to determine a causation with these results, they are a good indicator of a difference in behaviour and attitude if parents do not show any interest in what their children do online and reiterate the importance of parental engagement with these issues. Comments like "this is too difficult for parents, it's up to the platforms to resolve" are not borne out with this data.

As a final comparison, to see change over time, below is a comparison of significant differences between responses in 2018 and those in 2023. In general, there are few changes between these two different sets of respondents, which is another indication of the robustness and reliability of this data. However, there are a few changes that are of interest. Firstly, mobile phones and laptops have become increasingly popular, and tablets are not. Mobile gaming devices have essentially ceased to be a separate device

Table 5.27 No house rules "I think I spend too much time online"

I think I spend too much time online

	Strongly agree (%)	Agree (%)	No opinion (%)	Disagree (%)	Strongly disagree (%)
Yes	9.25	23.98	26.25	26.54	13.99
No	14.47	27.09	25.67	19.94	12.83
Difference	5.22	3.11	−0.58	−6.60	−1.16

Table 5.28 No house rules getting support

Who would you turn to if you were upset by something that happened online (please tick all that apply)?

	Friends (%)	Parents (%)	Other family member (%)	School/teacher (%)	Police (%)
Yes	55.93	86.73	43.12	33.58	16.65
No	68.10	74.67	32.98	23.62	15.85
Difference	12.17	−12.06	−10.14	−9.96	−0.80

(because of gaming on smartphones) and television is a more likely route for online interaction (Table 5.29).

We have also seen a general increase in how long young people spend online in an average day. Again, it is impossible to answer why this is, but this is a pre- and post-COVID comparison where a lot of young people's lives and educational interactions went online (Table 5.30).

When asked if they have seen anything online that is upsetting, there is a slight increase but this is not significant change (Table 5.31):

And there is a tendency for more young people to think that it is none of their parents' business what they do online, and there is greater worry

Table 5.29 Five-year difference devices

What do you use to go online? (please tick all you use)

	Mobile/ smart phone (%)	Laptop/ netbook (%)	Tablet (e.g. iPad) (%)	Home gaming devices (%)	Mobile gaming devices, (%)	Desktop pc (%)	Television (%)
2018 (n = 2267)	82.03	61.17	55.54	40.05	16.22	26.94	45.14
2023 (n = 1864)	87.18	70.42	38.95	46.88	0.00	26.89	59.16

Table 5.30 Five-year difference screen time

How much time do you spend online in an average day?

	Less than an hour (%)	One to three hours (%)	Between 3 and 6 hours (%)	More than 6 hours (%)
2018 (n = 2267)	20.87	45.92	23.91	9.30
2023 (n = 1864)	10.26	35.61	36.92	17.21

Table 5.31 Five-year difference upset online

Have you ever seen anything online that has made you feel upset?

	Yes (%)	No (%)
2018 (n = 2267)	30.33	69.67
2023 (n = 1864)	34.02	65.98

about spending too much time online, which is particularly interesting given the increase in screen time between the two year that are compared (Table 5.32).

There is also a slight increase in the application of house rules (Table 5.33): However, perhaps most telling is a particular response to the question regarding to whom they would disclose. The significant drop is disclosures in schools, which have reduced by almost 10%. Given how there is an expectation that schools provide a lot of safeguarding for young people, and have statutory duties for young people's safeguarding, including that online, it is a particular concern to see this clear drop and shows a further disconnect with a key stakeholder (Table 5.34).

Table 5.32 Five-year difference comparisons

It is none of my parents' business what I do online

	Strongly agree (%)	Agree (%)	No opinion (%)	Disagree (%)	Strongly disagree (%)
2018 (*n* = 2267)	7.63	15.27	24.53	32.88	19.69
2023 (*n* = 1864)	7.25	17.48	28.19	30.79	16.29
I think I spend too much time online					
2018 (*n* = 2267)	8.36	25.71	26.84	26.80	12.29
2023 (*n* = 1864)	11.23	29.84	27.78	23.55	7.60

Table 5.33 Five-year difference house rules

Are there any rules at home for using the internet?

	Yes (%)	No (%)
2018 (*n* = 2267)	59.95	40.05
2023 (*n* = 1864)	64.95	35.05

Table 5.34 Five-year difference getting support

Who would you turn to if you were upset by something that happened online (please tick all that apply)?

	Friends (%)	Parents (%)	Other family member (%)	School/teacher (%)	Police (%)
2018 (*n* = 2267)	66.98	79.58	37.55	31.18	17.03
2023 (*n* = 1864)	66.44	79.39	32.47	21.30	9.96

CONCLUSIONS

The chapter delves into the disconnect between grassroots evidence and policy direction concerning online harms, focusing particularly on the overlooked input of young people. It highlights that the concerns of youth are often misrepresented by policy makers who focus on extreme online content like self-harm and pornography, while young people are more troubled by everyday issues such as peer conflict, social media anxiety, and content informed by current affairs. The data from a survey of 16,000 young people reveals a preference for seeking help from peers rather than uninformed adults and the frustrations in not being able to disclose and get support. Equally, in contrast to the policy perspective that platforms should sort out all issues related to online harms, young people will not consider disclosure to platforms as viable route to resolve an online harms issue.

This further underscores the gap between young people's actual experiences and the assumptions of policy makers and adults. The data shows that most young people have positive online experiences, with the main causes of distress being peer abuse and exposure to upsetting current affairs, rather than the extreme content often highlighted in policy discussions as the driver for prohibitive measures. Young people expressed a need for adults, particularly parents and educators, to be more knowledgeable and supportive rather than punitive. The survey also highlights the discrepancy in attitudes and responses between young people and the adults responsible for their safeguarding, emphasizing the need for a more youth-centric approach in addressing online harms.

In this chapter and the preceding one, we have dug deep into a considerable evidence base to explore the aptitude of microsystem around the child regarding their place in the online harms ecosystem. And we can clearly see a disconnect between the macrosystem and the microsystem. While policy makers drive regulatory instruments into the microsystem, and provide national policy guidance around online safety, this does not necessarily result in better practice.

The increased safeguarding guidance in schools has some impact in terms of online safety policy and practice in these settings, but it also indicates the statutory guidance does not necessarily mean that schools will implement everything they are mandated to do. A lot of schools have policy in place but poorly trained staff and a lack of scrutiny from governors who are suitably poorly informed—even though it is their statutory duty to have training in place.

Engagement with families (another key stakeholder in the microsystem as highlighted in this chapter) is also not a top priority for schools with almost 20% doing nothing to promote online safety with parents. It would seem that schools will implement those requirements that require some, but not significant, effort (e.g. downloading a policy template and shaping that for the setting), but they are less likely to invest in long-term online safety strategies.

We also see a reduction in investment in the delivery of online safety education in secondary settings (even though they are mandated to deliver it) with evidence from ProjectEvolve that the teaching of anything related to digital literacy (and therefore aspects for understanding online harms) all but ends after primary school.

We can also see from this data that, without clear national guidance on what online safety training and education looks like, schools are free to pick and choose the topics they cover which might align with those subjects the teaching staff are more comfortable with. While some teachers are delivering a lot of education around these issues, there is a focus on topics away from technical knowledge with a focus on traditional online safety tropes (stranger danger, once its online its always online, etc.). We can also see that in what is assessed in schools around these topics. Once again, we should reiterate that good technical skills and knowledge are essential parts of risk mitigation online—if one can protect their resources and devices, they are reducing the risk of unauthorized access and, for example, the distribution of sensitive or intimate content.

In exploring the views of young people themselves, we can see that young people are engaged with online services and access in multiple ways, even those that might be considered by adults to be "illegal" for them to use. We also show clear evidence that most of the time most young people have positive online experiences, and their views do not reflect the moral panics and hyperbole that is often portrayed in the media and policy debates.

Young people are happy to disclose to adults when they are young, but this trust erodes as they get older and are more likely to be engaging in risky behaviour. This is frequently underpinned by a mistrust of adults' response and their knowledge of online incidents. This is reinforced with discussions with professionals conducted as part of the Headstart project which do indeed show that adults adopt prohibitive stances and make use of legal discourse to either shame or victim blame young people. Their views that disclosure can result in adults "freaking out" and making things worse are not without merit.

However, that is not to say that young people do not want engagement with those adults with safeguarding responsibilities. Young people are generally happy with house rules, and we can see from evidence that those who do have house rules generally spend less time online and are more likely to disclose to adults if they are upset by something. Those with no house rules (which might be an indicator of a lack of parental engagement?) spend more time online, engage with services at a younger age, and are more likely to turn to their peers for support.

Certainly, from discussions with young people they want adults to talk to and for them to provide support, but equally many do not have much confidence this will be the case in reality. They want teachers who will answer their questions and understand their concerns, and can offer help and support, they do not need saving from the "dark side of the internet". As we have stated above, most of the time most young people are having positive experiences online. They just need advice when upsetting things do occur. And what causes that upset is wide ranging and individualized, and not something that is easy to prohibit without blanket bans on access to mainstream media and online services.

Yet we can see that, as far as young people are concerned, things are not improving and they continue to receive poor education and a lack of support from adults, something they consider far more important than "holding platforms to account". Does this mean that industry should be disregarding as a stakeholder in online safeguarding? Of course not, they have many duties. However, we can show that change in legislation with a single stakeholder focus does little to improve the ecosystem for young people. It is, as a research and author who has written extensively about these issues, incredibly frustrating to see that the wishes of young people in research published since 2009 (Phippen & Brennan, 2020, ibid.) and that of other scholars (e.g. Bond, 2011; Ringrose et al., 2012; Setty, 2019) are still being ignored and an ideological obsession with "bringing big tech billionaires to heel" remains the priority, while young people are told they need to just stop doing bad things online because they're illegal. In the final part of this book, I will reflect on this frustration and make suggestions regarding why this remains the case, and how there might be a better way.

REFERENCES

Bond, E. (2011). The mobile phone= bike shed? Children, sex and mobile phones. *New Media & Society, 13*(4), 587–604.

OFCOM. (2024). *Children's media literacy report 2024.* Accessed October 2024, from https://www.ofcom.org.uk/siteassets/resources/documents/research-and-data/media-literacy-research/children/children-media-use-and-attitudes-2024/childrens-media-literacy-report-2024.pdf

Phippen, A. (2017). *Children's online behaviour and safety: Policy and rights challenges.* Springer.

Phippen, A., & Brennan, M. (2020). *Sexting and revenge pornography: Legislative and social dimensions of a modern digital phenomenon.* Routledge.

Ringrose, J., Gill, R., Livingstone, S., & Harvey, L. (2012). *A qualitative study of children, young people and 'sexting': A report prepared for the NSPCC.*

Setty, E. (2019). A rights-based approach to youth sexting: Challenging risk, shame, and the denial of rights to bodily and sexual expression within youth digital sexual culture. *International Journal of Bullying Prevention, 1*(4), 298–311.

CHAPTER 6

The Broken Online Safety Ecosystem

Abstract This chapter presents a critical analysis of the UK's online safety ecosystem, arguing that it has devolved into a safeguarding dystopia. Drawing on Bronfenbrenner's ecological systems theory, the chapter explores how disjointed interactions between policy makers, educational institutions, social services, and the media create a system that fails to meet the nuanced needs of young people. Through case studies, including incidents of victim-blaming and overreliance on punitive measures for teen sexting, the chapter demonstrates that the ecosystem prioritizes prohibitive and reactionary responses over empathetic, evidence-based support. By focusing narrowly on legislative and policy measures at the macrosystem level, stakeholders often neglect essential support within the microsystem and mesosystem, exacerbating mistrust among young people and diminishing their willingness to disclose online harms. Ultimately, the chapter advocates for a paradigm shift towards youth-centred approaches that prioritize supportive, informed engagement across all levels of the ecosystem to genuinely protect and empower young people online.

Keywords Online safety ecosystem • Safeguarding dystopia • Youth voice • Ecological systems theory • Victim-blaming

© The Author(s), under exclusive license to Springer Nature Switzerland AG 2025
A. Phippen, *Policy and Rights Challenges in Children's Online Behaviour and Safety, 2017–2023*,
https://doi.org/10.1007/978-3-031-80286-7_6

In the previous two chapters we have explored a considerable amount of empirical data to understand what is happening with one stakeholder in the ecosystem close to the child (schools) and also what young people themselves have disclosed about their online lives and their needs for support. Chapter 4 provided a detailed window into online safety policy and practice in schools, and showed schools demonstrating some of their statutory duties (in terms of having policies in place) but when it came to those less well defined in statutory guidance, there was less good practice, and almost a third of schools in the large sample have no training in place, even though they are mandated to do so. We can further see, from the exploration of ProjectEvolve, that education around these issues virtually disappears in secondary schools, when young people are engaging in more online services and need a greater understanding of risk. And furthermore, the choice of educational resources by teachers does not suggest a holistic approach to online safety (with "stranger danger" still writ large). At the same time the large amount of survey data in Chap. 5 shows that young people are asking for help, but not getting it. At the end of the chapter, the reduction in willingness to disclose to either teachers or police should they be worried about something online shows how relationships within the microsystems are breaking down.

In this pivotal chapter, which, on a personal level made me recognize how broken and dystopian the ecosystem has become, we turn a critical eye to recent events that expose the fractures within the online safety ecosystem, underscoring how a system designed to protect young people can fail those it aims to support, and how the policy space has little influence on this. As both an academic and active participant in this space, I've observed firsthand the gaps and systemic inefficiencies that emerge when adult stakeholders impose prohibitive measures without fully understanding the context or listening to young people's voices. The examples explored here highlight not only the failures within the microsystems directly surrounding the child but also the ineffective trickle-down impact of recent legislative initiatives.

One specific case, involving a young woman seeking support after a concerning online incident, provides a stark example of how adult biases, outdated legal frameworks, and poorly informed practices can lead to victim-blaming rather than genuine support. Despite the young person's decision to disclose her experience to a trusted adult, she faced a punitive response—treated more like an offender than a victim. This case, along with similar incidents, signals the systemic disconnect between the needs of young people and the responses of the adults and institutions around them. And furthermore, the disconnect between micro-, exo-, and macro-systems would predict that legislation that focuses almost exclusively on the macrosystems will do little to improve the needs of young people around online harms.

Through this analysis, we argue that the online safety ecosystem is fundamentally broken, held back by prohibitive mindsets, moral panics, a lack of meaningful inter-system communication and accountability, and a failure to engage with the evidence, should it conflict with the policy direction. We examine how the persistent divide between the macro-level legislative ambitions and the exo- and micro-level stakeholders in young people's lives often results in negative outcomes, particularly for vulnerable youth seeking guidance and protection. Ultimately, this chapter invites a re-evaluation of the ecosystem itself, arguing that without restructuring and a genuine commitment to listening to young people, new legislative measures may continue to miss the mark, leaving young people underserved and often unsupported.

The Failure of the Microsystems

In this chapter, which is pivotal in conclusions around the fact that the online safety ecosystem is broken, I will present a reflection on recent events that have highlighted how broken the online harms ecosystem has become. As I was writing this book, as is typical, I was engaged in the stakeholder space. I spend a lot of time speaking with stakeholders, feeding the ethnographic reflections upon the state of the sector and also, hopefully, providing, along with other academic colleagues, a progressive and thought-provoking voice that comes from an evidence base strongly invoiced by the youth voice and grassroots in general.

However, perhaps the most damning, and personally concerning, recent incident occurred recently at a college I support. I should stress prior to exploring this case that the young person involved in this case has consented for me to write about it, and she is currently being supported to attempt to achieve a better outcome. However, the current (at the time of writing) outcome demonstrates a failure of the microsystems in supporting a vulnerable young person who turned to adults for help and support and is pivotal in my arguments that the current ecosystem is broken and the new legislation will do little to support young people or listen to what they call for.

I was approached by the college because of what they referred to as a problematic safeguarding outcome by the local authority that they neither agreed with nor understood. When I asked for more details, I was told the following.

A young person (16) had come to pastoral support at the college because she was concerned about something that had occurred online. The college have an admirable pastoral and student support approach which encourages a "disclosure first" approach and, having spoken to many students at the college, one that the students believe in.[1]

The young woman disclosed to a safeguarding professional at the college that she had been "flirting" on messenger apps with the parent of a friend of hers (male, aged 40). She said she had known the man for a number of years and would be considered a friend of the family. Then, after much encouragement from him, she sent him an intimate image. However, once sent and she had reflected on it, she was concerned about what she had done and turned to the college for advice.

The college, quite correctly, said that because there was a potential criminal element at play, they would have to refer to the local authority. The local authority then liaised with police and at a case conference told the young women that because she had sent the parent an intimate image, she had broken the law and would be subject to an "Outcome 22" referral.

While the issues with the legislation around teen sexting are beyond the scope of this book, and explored elsewhere (Phippen & Brennan, 2020; Phippen & Bond, 2023), it is useful for context to provide an overview here. The legislation that is applied to teen sexting in the UK, the Protection of Children Act 1978 (UK Government, 1978). The foundation of the legislation makes it illegal for someone to generate and distribute an indecent image of a child. It is without question, if we are to consider the wording of the legislation, that in the event of self-production and voluntary sharing of an intimate image of themselves, the victim will

---

[1] In 2022, recognizing the post-COVID increases in mental health support need by young people, the college adopted a new approach to pastoral education and support. Rather than what tends to be traditionally done, which is to deliver pastoral education with class tutors, all of whom had varying levels of pastoral training and knowledge, the college recruited eight "Pastoral Support Tutors" who specialized in delivering pastoral education and would also be allocated to students in the college should there be a need for one-to-one support. Within a year of implementing this progressive, youth-centric approach, the number of disclosures in the college had trebled, showing the confidence the students had in disclosing and getting help and support.

also be perpetrator under this legislation. However, the legislation was introduced and debated in a time before the day when someone might have the technical capability to produce an image of themselves in a private setting and make use of a global communication network to distribute it to a consenting recipient. In the era where the legislation was established, the means to produce and distribute such imagery was costly and time-consuming and would be virtually impossible for the subject of the image to be the taker and distributor of the image.

From a punitive perspective, within the legislation teen sexting is unambiguously illegal under s1 PCA:

it is an offence for a person—

(a) to take, or permit to be taken [or to make], any indecent photograph [or pseudo-photograph] of a child. . .; or
(b) to distribute or show such indecent photographs [or pseudo-photographs]; or
(c) to have in his possession such indecent photographs [or pseudo-photographs], with a view to their being distributed or shown by himself or others; or
(d) to publish or cause to be published any advertisement likely to be understood as conveying that the advertiser distributes or shows such indecent photographs [or pseudo-photographs], or intends to do so.

While the legislation was updated in:

- s45 2003 Sexual Offences Act (UK Government, 2003a)

which extended the law such that the subject of the image could be under 18, from the previous under sixteen, therefore aligning with age of majority rather than age of consent.

And was updated further with

- s67 2015 Serious Crime Act (UK Government, 2015)

Where images may have been taken when the victim was under 18, prosecutors should consider whether any offences under section 1 of the Protection of Children Act 1978 (taking, distributing, possessing, or publishing indecent photographs of a child) or under section 160 of the

Criminal Justice Act 1988 (UK Government, 1988) (possession of an indecent photograph of a child) have been committed.

As explored in Phippen and Bond (2023), with growing evidence of young people being criminalized for self-produced imagery, in winter 2016, the College of Policing issued its own guidance, which allows a sexting incident to be reported and recorded, without the child ending up with a criminal record. The guidance was issued on something referred to as an "Outcome 21" response:

> Further investigation, resulting from the crime report, which could provide evidence sufficient to support formal action being taken against the suspect is not in the public interest—police decision.

The Crown Prosecution Service, who decide if cases go to trial, also raised concerns whether most consensual teen sexting incidents would pass the public interest test. While this was viewed as a youth-centric progressive step forward, further reading of the guidance raised some concerns this would not necessarily be the case. In the guidance it was suggested that the following is read out to the child and/or parents to clarify the use of outcome 21 recording:

> You/Your child has been recorded on police systems against (add crime type) in line with Home Office crime recording rules. After consideration of all relevant factors, a decision has been made that no further action will be taken by the police in this instance. <Your child> has not been convicted or cautioned for any offence connected with this investigation.

In the event that a future "Enhanced Disclosure and Barring Service" (DBS) check is required it is unlikely that this record will be disclosed unless you/your child are investigated or have further action taken against you/them in the future which could suggest a relevant pattern of behaviour.

In the evolution of the application of criminal justice outcomes, we started to also see the application of "Outcome 22" recording to teen sexting. Outcome 22 is a different approach to the application of Outcome 21. Guidance produced by the National Police Chief's Council in 2019 defined Outcome 22 as:

Outcome Type 22:
  Diversionary, educational or intervention activity, resulting from the crime report, has been undertaken and it is not in the public interest to take any further action.

An outcome 22 was a general "outcome" that could be recorded against all manner of crimes, it was not specifically developed for teen sexting. It was viewed as means to deal with low-level crimes where use of a "diversionary activity" could be used so that no further action needed to take place. Guidance on Outcome 22 at the time presented a confused picture of its application to teen sexting issues, stating on one page that it should not be applied to teen sexting incidents then on the subsequent page saying that you can if you want to.

Therefore, by the letter of the law according to those professionals dealing with the case, they correctly believed that the application of this outcome was appropriate in this case. And because the young women when first spoken to said she did not feel like she had been coerced into sending the image (even though the behaviour of the adult would suggest otherwise), the conclusion of the police was that the abuser had done nothing wrong so there would be no further action against him. So, he was not spoken to as part of the "investigation". The young woman was assigned a social worker to support her with the diversionary intervention, and a sexual violence worker.

The young woman, when told of this outcome, raised concerns with the college regarding how she had been treated yet felt powerless to challenge it (a 16-year-old young woman verses social care and police services). She told the college she would not disclose any further concerns because the outcome was not one of support but of criminalization, and she was made to feel like she was the one who had done something wrong.

The college contacted me for advice, with the top-level details of the case and my response, unsurprisingly, was that it sounded like a completely inappropriate response to this disclosure. Upon further conversation with the college, I was told that they had asked their local community support police officer for advice on this but was told "this is above my pay grade", and discussions with the social worker had reinforced the view that what the young woman had done was wrong and this was the best result for her. When asked why there was no further action against the parent, they were simply told that this is what the police told the social care team. At no point was the young woman spoken to by the police, all details of the case were communicated to police by the social care professionals.

I further asked if the Outcome 22 was an educational intervention and if so, who was delivering this. The college had asked the social care team, who were not sure but thought that might be something the sexual violence worker might do.

At this point I asked if the young woman would like to talk to me, because it might be good for her to have someone independent to speak to and someone who had good awareness of the law in this context. After a while the college said that she would like to speak, so I met with her, and have subsequently met with her on several other occasion.

Within a ten-minute conversation with the young woman, I discovered that prior to her sending the parent an image, he had sent her a connection request on Snapchat, sent her many messages flattering her, then sent an explicit image to encourage her to do similar. And when the young woman told his son about what had happened, the parent called her to attempt to coerce her into saying she made it up. While she did say that at the time she had told the social worker that she did not feel coerced, looking at it as she had just described it did sound like she had. I was surprised to discover no one had asked this young woman these questions before.

When I asked whether anyone had done any educational work with her, she said she had not. When I asked whether the sexual violence worker was treating her as a victim or a perpetrator, she said she felt it was a mix of the two.

While she said that she appreciated by the letter of the law she had done something wrong by sharing an intimate image with someone else when she was under 18, she did not understand how she could be told she had done something wrong by sending yet he had done nothing wrong even though he had encouraged it and was in possession. Equally, she said that she could not be confident he would not do this with others and her concern was that if he did this, it was reported and a different police response resulted in him being spoken to, there was no record that he had done similar with her.

From my perspective, I was very much in agreement that if she distributed, he would be in possession, and also felt that she was clearly groomed. And while the legislation for sexual communication with a child is limited to minors under 16 (UK Government, 2003b), there is also an Inchoate offence[2] (Herring et al., 1998) where it could certainly be strongly argued that this adult incited this young woman to commit this offence. The

[2] https://www.cps.gov.uk/legal-guidance/inchoate-offences [Accessed October 2024]

young woman said that she did not want this person arrested and jailed, but equally she felt that for the police to say that he had done nothing wrong, and there was no need to record the incident for him, was imbalanced and unfair given her treatment by the samr professionals. It is very difficult to disagree.

Finally, when asked about any educational intervention, the young woman said that this was not something she had experienced in her conversation with either social worker and sexual violence support worker.

We are dealing with a case where a young woman, coerced into sending an adult an intimate image, was treated like an offender by several professionals who, at no stage, took the time to explore the case in more detail and understand the context in which the image exchange was occurring. Far easier, it would seem, to recognize the prohibitive mindset that, regardless of extenuating circumstances, any young person who does this has broken the law. And if they are unlikely to make a fuss, record as an Outcome 22 and send them on their way, regardless of the potential for this to be returned in a criminal record check in the future. Perhaps the most frustrating thing for me is that, aside from the college who have been excellent in supporting the young woman, any interests in the best outcomes for her have been dismissed as too difficult and an Outcome 22 is far less hassle for the professionals to put in place. I should stress, by way of observation, that this is a local authority who claim to be "children's rights focused" and all children's workforce practitioners have "ask me about Article 3" in their email signatures. Once again highlighting how rights frameworks, while used in conversation, are not applied in practice.

When presenting the first case study at a national talk at a Safer Internet Day conference in 2024, I was approached by a senior police officer from a different part of the country, who cautiously said, "that wasn't us was it?" When I confirmed it was not, he went on to say that it was indeed a fairly child-centric policing, but he could see why it happened and would simply be the case that it was dealt with by a busy low-ranking officer trying to clear it from his caseload as quickly as possible.

During dealing with this case, I was also made aware of another issue being dealt with by the safeguarding team. In this case, they were supporting a young person in foster care with her time at the college. During a safeguarding meeting both the foster family and the social care team talked about how to spot check the young person's mobile phone "in order to make sure she's not up to anything bad". Perhaps most concerning was this was discussed in the open with no one raising concerns about the serious impact on the young person's privacy and a complete failure to consider this against the best interests of the child and specifically impacts upon their articles 13 (Freedom of Expression) and 16 (right to privacy) rights. Just to reiterate, this is from practitioners who claim to have the best interests of the child at the centre of every decision they make.

Both of the cases above, the first so pivotal in my belief of the disconnect between micro and macrosystems, are certainly, it would seem, not unusual. Indeed, while writing this book the BBC ran a similar story in a different part of the country.[3] In this case, a teenage abuse victim criticized Wiltshire Police and Swindon Borough Council for failing to protect him after he disclosed he was coerced into sending someone who would eventually be convicted of multiple child sexually abuse offences (so serious he ended up with a twenty-year prison sentence) and intimate image. However, when he complained to the police, they initially dismissed his claims and even threatened him with prosecution because by producing the image he was breaking the law. The local authority has acknowledged safeguarding failures, apologized, and promised procedural improvements. The victim emphasized his betrayal by authorities and called for systemic changes to protect children more effectively. At the time of reporting of this case, there was an internal investigation into police conduct ongoing.

In this book we have spent a lot of time exploring the legislative frameworks that are now in place, to much political and media excitement, to better protect young people from online harms. In this case, is there anything in this legislation that would help her?

Clearly not, these changes occurred, from an ecosystem viewpoint, far away from the young person and the professionals around her, and focused almost entirely on other stakeholders in the macrosystem. While there have, over the years (Phippen & Brennan, 2020), been calls by politicians for mobile providers to install algorithms to detect if a minor has taken an intimate image and prevent it from being transmitted (which opens a collected of ethical issues [Phippen & Bond, 2020]), there is little that platform liability or safety by design can do to prevent this young person being let down by those adults around her in the microsystems, who both failed to listen to her and applied their own biased interpretations of events.

While the macrosystem stakeholders are battling for column inches and political notoriety, this young woman was failed by those in the microsystem and exosystem who, instead of considering her best interests,

[3] https://www.bbc.co.uk/news/articles/cjrdz0qegg3o [Accessed October 2024]

consistently applied prohibitive and victim-blaming attitudes. In this case at best, they have treated a victim of abuse as an offender, and made her mistrusting of disclosing future incident, as well as potentially impacting on her future career goals. At worst, they have provided an environment where they ignored the abuse of a minor and enabled the abuser to do similar with others.

This case, coming on a top of experiences that highlighted to me that those around the child are perhaps not as well informed as they could be, and would be all too willing to bring their own biases and opinions to safeguarding judgements that certainly are nowhere near the best interests of the child and result of poor, and long-term, outcomes for young people.

Or, the ecosystem is broken.

And this "new class" of legislation will do little to rectify this.

Extending the Safeguarding Dystopia

In this chapter, in bringing together a lot of the exploration around the ecosystem, and reflecting upon what young people tell us, and with particular focus on recent empirical work, we argue that the ecosystem is broken. And it is broken in two ways—the failure of mesosystems and the sunk cost policy direction with no end goal in the macrosystem.

Firstly, we are clear from the explorations in Chaps. 4 and 5 that there is very little impact from the exosystem into the microsystems. The four key players in the macrosystem engage in an existential battle to "do more" and demand the eradication of harms by those who implement the platforms upon which they take place. The media inform these policy debates while trying to generate traffic and media profile through stoking moral panics around online harms, while certainly not adopting a critical perspective or evidence-led view, the impact of this upon the microsystems is rarely anything other causing disconnects between young people and adults close to them, or actually directing them towards the harms to which they claim to wish to protect them (as can be shown with the Momo panic in Chap. 3). While we have not, in detail, explored the role of the charitable/non-governmental organizations in these interactions, again in Chaps. 2 and 3 we have highlighted how there will be, within this stakeholder group, some efforts to promote the moral panics, rather than bringing criticality and evidence to these debates.

In the case of legislators, the macrosystem should have a role to play in developing legislation that is mindful of a young person's (and, arguably, any online user) needs and platforms should, clearly, provide tools and support for those who are concerned about something that is happening on these platforms and, more importantly, where platforms are still lacking, respond to these needs in an open and transparent manner. And they should also be mindful of the attitude and ideologies framed as the macrosystem, particularly drawing upon rights frameworks such as the UN Convention of the Rights of the Child and the European Convention on Human Rights, when making policy and technical decisions. However, our discussions around political debate (more of which will be drawn upon in this chapter) would suggest that the focus lies more on political posturing than appreciating the complexities of how we tackle online harms. While there is clearly goodwill on the part of some policy makers in this space, adopting reductionist views and prohibitive goals does little to appreciate the needs of young people (and there is little evidence on listening to young people if one explores the development of the Online Safety Act 2023) with a focus on "bringing big tech to heel" and imposing "huge fines" seems to distort the purported goal, which is to help young people have positive experiences online (which, for the majority of the time, most do). With so little in this legislation, or the majority of previous policy approaches to tackling online harms, that centres on the responsibilities of other stakeholders in addressing online safety, there are few opportunities to engage those stakeholders in the microsystems with anything other than an expectation that this can, and should, be resolved by the platforms. And what resolution looks like is prohibition.

A fundamental aspect of Bronfenbrenner's theory is the mesosystem that exist between the microsystems. According to Bronfenbrenner, a mesosystem is the interconnection between the various microsystems in a child's life. Microsystems are the immediate environments in which the child interacts, such as family, school, peer groups, and neighbourhood. The mesosystem is essentially a system of microsystems and involves the interactions between these environments.

For example, a mesosystem might include the relationship between a child's parents and their teachers. How these two environments (home and school) interact and communicate can significantly influence the child's development. Positive and supportive interactions between these microsystems can lead to a more cohesive and nurturing developmental environment for the child.

Yet, in our exploration of the evidence in Chaps. 4 and 5, there is significant support to the view that these mesosystems are not working together, and, drawing upon the evidence in this book and extensive qualitative work in the last few years (Phippen & Street, 2022), there within those microsystems are in tension. For example, teachers tell us that they cannot be responsible for policing what young people do on their devices 24/7. And parents tell us it is too complicated for them, with familiar refrains such as "they know more than me about this stuff". And the 360 Degree Safe data in Chap. 4 shows a significant minority of schools who do nothing to interact with parents regarding online safety matters at all.

However, perhaps the clearest example of the broken mesosystems is illustrated by the case at the above, this is a clear demonstration of the total breakdown in mesosystems and a failure for exo- and microsystem to comprehensively, coherently, and collectively respond in the best interests of the child. We can further reinforce this view with a more detailed exploration of how this prohibitive mindset occurs due to the failures of the mesosystems.

Legislation, developed in 1978 to ensure young people are protected in the manufacture of what was referred to at the time as, somewhat problematically, child pornography, is applied in a contemporary context in a manner for which it never intended. The Protection of Children Act 1978 was introduced as a private members bill with the best of intentions by Cyril Townsend, MP. The title of the bill makes it clear this piece of legislation is intended to protect children, in the case of the bill from the exploitation of children in the production of pornography by adult abusers. In its introduction to the House of Commons, Mr Townsend stated:

> We acted to prevent abuse of little children as chimney sweeps and in the factories. We acted to prevent their abuse in dark satanic mills and deep down in the mines. Shall we act today to prevent their abuse in child pornography?

Clearly, the intention is to protect children from exploitation. While the debates around the bill were long and detailed (explored in more detail in Phippen & Brennan, 2020) at no point in the discussions was it suggested that this might be something enacted upon a minor from another minor or that the subject of the image was also the taker and distributor of the image. In the late 1970s there is no reason to suggest anyone entertained the idea that in the future technology would be sufficiently advanced for an individual to take an intimate image of themselves and distribute it to peers using mass communication networks.

The growth of young people making use of digital technology to exchange nudes/intimate images results in adult stakeholders in child safeguarding to determine how best to tackle this issue. The (legally correct) application of the Protection of Children Act 1978 to these issues means that a prohibitive message can be developed to inform young people that if they are doing this they are breaking the law, and cases in the criminal justice system picked up by the media highlight this. Educational messages use these stories to point out how engaging in sharing intimate images under the age of 18 can result in a criminal charge, so don't do it.

The stakeholders in this case, all informed by prohibitive messaging and moral panics perpetuated in the exosystems, have decided, instead of exploring the complexities of the case, or placing the best interests of the child at the centre of their decisions, that the young person should not have done the act of sending an intimate image, and should therefore be punished for it.

As discussed in Chap. 6, the introduction of diversions from the criminal justice system evolved directly as a result of one of the stakeholder in the exosystem (the police) seeing how problematic the application of this legislation was to minors exchanging intimate images and how victims of abuse might be caught up in applying "the letter of the law".

Yet the complexity of the current legal approach has not impacted upon the educational messages (again, illustrating a break down in the mesosystems) which remain steadfastly aligned to the "don't do it, it's illegal" mindset. And the impact of these educational messages is severe, resulting in young people unwilling to disclose harm (e.g. in the event of non-consensual sharing) or, if they do disclose, not receiving any support in rectifying the issues they are facing.

But when we explore authentic youth voice in the literature (Ringrose & Renold, 2010; Hunt, 2021; Setty, 2023; Setty et al., 2024) on the sexting phenomenon, it is almost unheard of for young people to call for prohibitive legislation and "bans". They are far more likely to ask for more detail on the current legislation, how it relates to people their age, and the need to better control not the act of sending an intimate image but the non-consensual further sharing of the image.

Is it because it is easier to tell a child not to do it and make use of the law to scare them, rather than understanding the nuance and context around the acts of exchanging images and the relative impact based upon these factors? A simple random sample of disclosures from Everyone's Invited (Sara, 2022), a website where child victims of sexual harassment and abuse in schools anonymously disclosed their experiences, easily found further cases of young people talking about these prohibitive messages and lack of support, including:

- A young person who had intimate images shared non-consensually at the age of 13, who still suffers anxiety issues at the age of 21 as a result. The victim states that she blames herself.
- A young person pressured into sending nudes at the age of 12, who did so because she thought "that's how dating is these days".
- A young person who, after a sexual encounter with a peer, with the peer then claiming he'd taken images non-consensually and shared them with his friends. When she was sent the images, they were not of her, but when she disclosed the abuse to a teacher, instead of support they received a lecture on the dangers and legalities of sharing nudes.

These disclosures reflect the conversations I have had with young people, and certainly provide validity to the fact that the case discussed in Chap. 6 is certainly not a one-off. As we have seen in Chap. 5 with the change in attitudes to disclosure as they get older, young people become mistrusting of those in the microsystems in their teenage years. This is backed up by many discussions with young people who, when asked who they would disclose to if someone had non-consensually shared images of them, mostly say there was no way they would speak to a teacher or parent. Far better, and less "risky", to talk it through with peers.

This message is reinforced by police, who are often called into schools to deliver assemblies on this topic. The message given to young people in these assemblies, delivered by a police officer in uniform is, "don't do it, it's illegal", alongside further statements like a young person could end up on the sex offenders register and unable to travel due to visa issues for people with criminal records.

As a result of interactions across the microsystems, the prohibitive mindset prevails into other stakeholders, such as social care and becomes prevalent in those settings.

Young people who have received this prohibitive education move into the children's workforce and, with a dearth of effective training (as discussed in Chaps. 4 and 6), take these views into safeguarding judgements they must make.

And as explored in Phippen and Bond (2023), while there is a reduction in entry of young people into the criminal justice system for these behaviours, Outcome 21 and 22 referrals are rife, and seem to follow no consistent path. Their application varies across different police forces with some applying them liberally and some not at all. For those adopting an Outcome 22 route, there is no guidance of what a diversion or educational intervention should look like, and practitioners will still use prohibitive resources to reinforce the point that what the young person did was wrong, and they are lucky to have not been arrested.

At the same time the child, in the middle of the ecosystem and supposedly supported by these adults in the microsystems around them, has been receiving these prohibitive messages throughout their school lives. In some cases, such as the one in Chap. 6, the impact of being groomed results in them receiving an Outcome 22. More generally, these messages are also known by abusers. So if someone is groomed into sending intimate images, and are a minor, the abuser now, as a result of this prohibitive approach, has more power over their victim and can, firstly, tell them they cannot tell anyone because what they have done is illegal and, secondly, can coerce them into further acts as a result. And the young person, having been in receipt of these prohibitive messages, "knows" the abuser is correct, and therefore becomes more vulnerable as a result.

We also know that these messages impact on adult life, and previous work with the Revenge Porn Helpline in the UK, who support adult victims of image-based abuse, tell us (Phippen & Brennan, 2020) that many victims will say "I know I shouldn't have sent the images" or "I know it's my fault" which clearly correlates with the prohibitive messages some would have experienced in school.

However, to contrast this with the development of legislation to protect adults from what is sometimes problematically referred to as "Revenge Pornography" and more correctly referred to as image-based abuse, the contrast could not be more stark. In terms of "supporting" young people, they are told that they should not take or share intimate images because they are illegal (while not having it explained to them this is based upon legislation from 1978, and there are a number of sticking plasters over this approach because it is widely acknowledged by stakeholders that the legislation is not being used in the purpose for which it was developed). However, in terms of adult image-based abuse things have kept up with technological changes and an 18-year-old who exchanges images with a partner, and whose partner then shares them further without consent, will be protected in law, and the partner subject to prosecution under section 33 of the Criminal Justice and Courts Act 2015, updated in the Domestic Abuse Act 2021 and the Online Safety Act 2023 2024. A 17-year-old in the same scenario would, in theory, risk arrest (or threat of arrest) themselves for doing similar. Which does beg the question—why is it that so much (positive) effort has been placed in protecting adult victims of image-based abuse while still apply the ineffective (and certainly in some cases harmful) "just say no" messages for young people?

Perhaps a more realistic model of the ecosystem, based upon Bronfenbrenner's theoretical foundations, is represented below (Fig. 6.1):

In this model, firstly there is a break in all the systems. Rather than working together in the best interests of the child, those stakeholders within these systems, with poor knowledge and a wealth of personal moral positions and biases, decide they know what is best for the young person, and this usually centres on prohibition. While some information might flow between them, the macrosystem seems more focused on interactions with stakeholders within this layer, rather than engaging with, and listening to, concerns from young people and the microsystems. Coupled with a prohibitive narrative and a view that online harms can be prevented if only the providers did more, this does not encompass the microsystems

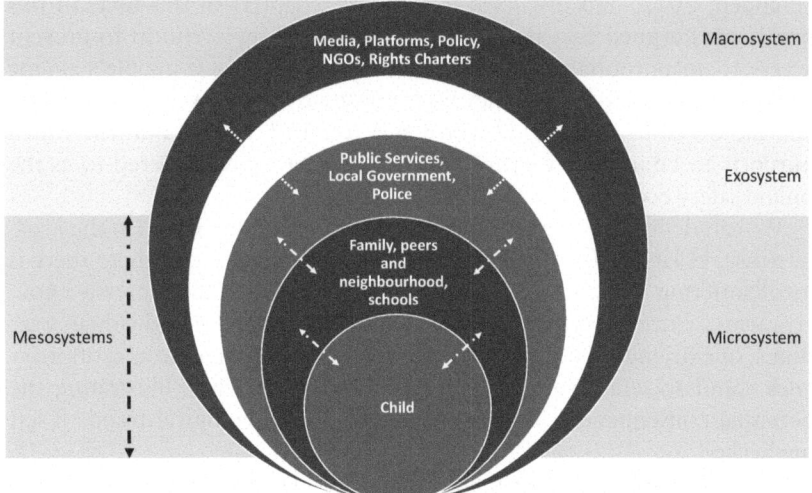

Fig. 6.1 The broken ecosystem

with evidence informed or child-centric view on how to tackle online harms. Furthermore, the mesosystems across the microsystem are also broken, and represent both a failure of communication and a conflict across the microsystem but also failing to incorporate the needs of the child of their best interests in responses to disclosure or calls for support.

In essence, there is virtually a vacuum between the macrosystem and the other systems. While stakeholders in the macrosystem battle and new law is developed with threats of bringing a stakeholder "to heel" with threats of "massive fines", the reality is, there is nothing to reach into the exo- and microsystems. While there has been, and will continue to be, a great deal of activity at this level, there is minimal transfer to the other systems and certainly there is little in the new legislation that empathizes with young people's wishes. Instead, these stakeholders are left with poor training and knowledge, and responses to moral panics fed by both the media and policy makers, which does little to make them realize the crucial role they have to play in addressing online harms. At the start of this book, I used a quote from a 17-year-old about how adults make things worse. In the case studies I have presented in this chapter, this is very much confirmed.

In bringing this discussion to a close, I return to the concept of the safeguarding dystopia introduced in the previous volume of this series (Phippen, 2017) and discussed in the early chapters of this text. In this first book I argued that the use of technological intervention to prevent access to inappropriate content and to monitor young people's online activities in order to ensure they were safe are dystopia in that their rights, and life outcomes, are made worse as a result of an environment which purports to be in their best interest (something I have referred to as the online safety ecosystem in this book).

We can define a dystopian society, drawing from literature (in the artistic sense, [Claeys, 2010]), as an imagined society or world where there is great suffering or injustice, typically one characterized by oppressive governments, extreme environmental degradation, loss of individual freedoms, or extreme economic inequality. Dystopias often serve as cautionary tales about societal issues taken to their worst extremes, illustrating the potential consequences of political, social, or technological trends if left unchecked.

Dystopian literature, as we understand it today, began to take shape in the late nineteenth and early twentieth centuries, inspired by societal shifts, technological advances, and reactions to political ideologies. Several authors are considered pioneers of the genre, each bringing unique perspectives to the depiction of bleak, authoritarian, or nightmarish societies.

- H.G. Wells—Often recognized as one of the early influences, H.G. Wells introduced dystopian themes in works like *The Time Machine* (1895), which depicted a future society divided sharply along class lines. His work speculated on the dangers of unchecked technological advancements and class inequalities.
- Yevgeny Zamyatin—Zamyatin's *We* (written in 1920, published in 1924) is one of the first novels to embody the dystopian genre that evolved, portraying a society governed by oppressive surveillance, conformity, and loss of individual freedom. We directly influenced later authors, notably George Orwell.
- Aldous Huxley—*Brave New World* (1932) is another foundational work in dystopian literature. Huxley created a world of genetic engineering, mind control, and consumerism, offering a critique of both social and political trends. His work highlighted the dangers of sacrificing individuality for stability and superficial happiness.
- George Orwell—With *1984* (1949), Orwell cemented the dystopian genre in modern literature. His depiction of totalitarianism, propaganda, and psychological manipulation has become one of the most influential works of dystopian literature, profoundly shaping our understanding of oppressive regimes.

Therefore, it might be argued that claiming the current online safety ecosystem is dystopian and hyperbole. However, I would argue that the hallmarks are there, particularly if we draw upon evidence presented within this text.

A safeguarding dystopia would be a society in which efforts to protect individuals, especially vulnerable groups, become so extreme or intrusive that they end up harming personal freedoms, rights, privacy, and autonomy. In this type of dystopia, the well-intended goal of protecting people from harm is pursued with excessive control, surveillance, or regulation, often leading to an oppressive environment.

For example, constant monitoring of young people's actions, restrictions on personal choices, and harsh punishments for minor infractions could be justified in the name of safeguarding. Conversely, this approach erodes trust, autonomy, and the sense of personal responsibility, creating a rigid and fearful society, or population within that society (in our case, young people).

In my original discussions about the safeguarding dystopia, I argued that technology surveillance and control of access to content and participation were the reasons that it was dystopian. In the analysis of the ecosystem presented in this book, I would argue that there are far more dystopian elements, such as a restriction in the education young people are calling for (and have been calling for over many years), policy directions that dismiss the youth voice and instead believe that blanket bans are better than the individualized response, and media narratives that inform policy with little basis in evidence also have their role in the safeguarding dystopia.

I do not see this because of totalitarian regimes that are often described in dystopian fiction. However, the banality of decisions made, whether this is the implementation of policies or actions carried out by professionals show how we can sleep walk into a safeguarding dystopia. I am not suggesting that the political classes are implementing these problematic legal approaches because they want children to be harmed. However, their sunk costs motivate a policy direction that, due to prohibitive nature, do not consider the unintended consequences of their proposals.

And I am sure that those professionals whose decisions impacted so negatively upon the young person at the start of this chapter did not do so because they did not care. However, due to poor decisions, a lack of training and knowledge, and personal moral biases, the impact upon this young person was undoubtedly negative and harmful. A young person being groomed by an adult ending up with a criminal record is undoubtedly a vignette in dystopian fiction. A vulnerable young person in foster care being told that to ensure they are safe, they need to have devices monitored and checked, and therefore they have no right to privacy, is equally dystopian. The impact on rights should not be dismissed as justifications in concern for their welfare. And, ultimately, this approach will do little to improve outcomes for the young person, it will just make them more secretive and less likely to disclosure should something of concern occur. In these cases, the ecosystem around the child, even though comprising adults who claims to have their best interests as a priority, resulted in outcomes for the vulnerable young person that negatively impacted upon their rights and life chances.

More broadly, the prevailing "online safety" policy discussions in 2024 centre (as we discussed in Chap. 2) on the prevention of access to smartphones and social media by young people. Using a popular science book (that has not undergone peer review) as a justification for these views, where politicians are looking for evidence to support their ideological position, while ignoring the wealth of literature that does not aim to make such crude causations (e.g. Przybylski & Weinstein, 2017; Orben, 2020; Vuorre et al., 2021) is undoubtedly dystopian in vision. I am sure the next volume of this series will reflect upon how these policies were ultimately unenforceable and young people's mental health issues did not suddenly and miraculously improve.

The ecosystem we have explored is not dystopian because just it takes away children's rights through technology, it completely ignores their wishes and develop an ecosystem for that is convenient for adults, not the young people at its centre. Returning to the UN CRC, respect for the views of the child (enshrined in article 12) are noticeably absent.

Conclusions

In concluding this chapter, we confront a disheartening truth: the online safety ecosystem, as it currently functions, often exacerbates the very harms it claims to prevent. Throughout this exploration, case studies have underscored how legislation, driven more by political posturing than by evidence, fails to address the nuanced realities of young people's digital lives. As a result, young people find themselves marginalized by policies that emphasize prohibition and punishment over protection and genuine support. This safeguarding dystopia erodes their autonomy, overlooks their voices, and in many cases, even deepens their vulnerability.

The opening case study illustrates the ecosystem's failings in poignant detail. Here, a minor, manipulated by an adult, found herself treated as a criminal, not a victim. This outcome reflects an ecosystem that has come to prioritize regulatory compliance and adult convenience over the well-being of the young people it aims to protect. And her experiences are certainly not unique, her experiences are a sadly logical outcome from an ecosystem applying out-of-date law to young people's online experiences. Legal frameworks that criminalize self-produced imagery were developed in an era before digital communication yet, when uncritically applied, often without consideration for the drastically different social and techno-logical context that young people navigate today. In situations like this, policies that were once meant to shield children from harm now serve as blunt instruments, wielded without sensitivity to the personal, social, and developmental dynamics at play.

The systemic failures detailed here expose a gap not only in policy but in professional practice, where those closest to young people—the microsystem stakeholders—are ill-equipped, undertrained, or misguided in responding to complex safeguarding issues. This disconnect is clearly evident in the mesosystem breakdown, where communication between key stakeholders—for example, schools, social services, law enforcement—often collapses under prohibitive policies or punitive biases. The lack of cohesive guidance and meaningful dialogue between these groups creates environments where young people are discouraged from disclosing concerns, fearing judgement or punishment instead of receiving constructive support.

More broadly, the macro-level legislative focus on preventing access to digital platforms often disregards the fundamental rights of young people. The ecosystem, as it stands, neglects to respect young people's right to privacy, autonomy, expression, education, and participation and instead opting for restrictive measures and generalized prohibitions that alienate them from adults and create mistrust. Rather than empowering young people to navigate digital spaces responsibly, current policies perpetuate a cycle of mistrust, where digital engagement is increasingly viewed with suspicion. The common refrain of "don't do it, it's illegal" does nothing to address the underlying complexities of digital interactions or equip young people with the tools to manage their online lives safely and thoughtfully.

As policy makers continue to prioritize top-down mandates, the ecosystem's inherent contradictions only deepen. The wider legislative narrative persists in casting online platforms as solely responsible for preventing harm, ignoring the critical roles of parents, educators, and social services in shaping young people's online experiences. Platforms may be expected to "do more" to curb online harms, yet systemic accountability at the micro- and exosystem levels remains sparse, leaving young people underserved. This approach fails to address the ecosystem's real issues, creating a vacuum where responsibility is pushed onto platforms while the foundational safeguards in young people's immediate environments are left wanting.

Moving forward, it is essential to rebuild this ecosystem, re-centring it around the actual needs and perspectives of young people, with their voice clearly heard. Rather than adopting simplistic, prohibitive policies, stakeholders must be open to more nuanced and empathetic approaches that incorporate a broad range of stakeholders. For instance, involving youth in policy-making, prioritizing education over punishment, and equipping professionals with up-to-date, youth-centred training would allow for a system that responds dynamically to young people's realities. Creating mechanisms that foster genuine inter-system collaboration, where schools, families, social services, and digital platforms engage in shared responsibility, could rebuild trust and ensure that safeguarding efforts genuinely serve young people's best interest far more effectively than prohibition and platform scapegoating will achieve.

References

Claeys, G. (2010). The origins of dystopia: Wells, Huxley and Orwell. In G. Claeys (Ed.), *The Cambridge companion to utopian literature*. Cambridge University Press.

Herring, J., Cremona, M., Herring, J., & Cremona, M. (1998). Inchoate offences. *Criminal Law*, 323–341.

Hunt, J. (2021). *Sex Ed for grown-ups: How to talk to children and young people about sex and relationships*. Routledge.

Orben, A. (2020). Teenagers, screens and social media: A narrative review of reviews and key studies. *Social Psychiatry and Psychiatric Epidemiology, 55*(4), 407–414.

Phippen, A. (2017). *Children's online behaviour and safety: Policy and rights challenges*. Springer.

Phippen, A., & Bond, E. (2020). Image recognition in child sexual exploitation material—Capabilities, ethics and rights. *Policing in the Era of AI and Smart Societies*, 179–198.

Phippen, A., & Bond, E. (2023). *Policing teen sexting – Supporting children's rights while applying the law*. Palgrave Macmillan.

Phippen, A., & Brennan, M. (2020). *Sexting and revenge pornography: Legislative and social dimensions of a modern digital phenomenon*. Routledge.

Phippen, A., & Street, L. (2022). *Online resilience and wellbeing in young people*. Springer.

Przybylski, A. K., & Weinstein, N. (2017). A large-scale test of the Goldilocks hypothesis: Quantifying the relations between digital-screen use and the mental well-being of adolescents. *Psychological Science, 28*(2), 204–215.

Ringrose, J., & Renold, E. (2010). *Boys, girls and performing normative violence in schools: A gendered critique of bully discourses. Children behaving badly? Peer violence between children and young people* (pp. 181–195).

Sara, S. (2022). *Everyone's invited*. Simon and Schuster.

Setty, E. (2023). Risks and opportunities of digitally mediated interactions: Young people's meanings and experiences. *Journal of Youth Studies*, 1–19.

Setty, E., Ringrose, J., & Hunt, J. (2024). From 'harmful sexual behaviour' to 'harmful sexual culture': Addressing school-related sexual and gender-based violence among young people in England through 'post-digital sexual citizenship'. *Gender and Education*, 1–19.

UK Government. (1978). *Protection of Children Act 1978 Section 1*. Accessed October 2024, from https://www.legislation.gov.uk/ukpga/1978/37/section/1

UK Government. (1988). *Criminal Justice Act 1988 Section 160*. Accessed October 2024, from https://www.legislation.gov.uk/ukpga/1988/33/section/160

UK Government. (2003a). *Sexual Offences Act 2003 Section 45*. Accessed October 2024, from https://www.legislation.gov.uk/ukpga/2003/42/section/45

UK Government. (2003b). *Sexual Offences Act 2003 Section 15A*. Accessed October 2024, from https://www.legislation.gov.uk/ukpga/2003/42/section/15A

UK Government. (2015). *Serious Crime Act 2015 Section 67*. Accessed October 2024, from https://www.legislation.gov.uk/ukpga/2015/9/section/67

Vuorre, M., Orben, A., & Przybylski, A. K. (2021). There is no evidence that associations between adolescents' digital technology engagement and mental health problems have increased. *Clinical Psychological Science, 9*(5), 823–835.

CHAPTER 7

Conclusions and Predictions for the Future of Online Safety Policy

Abstract This concluding chapter reflects on the systemic flaws and persistent challenges within online safety policy, particularly regarding its alignment with young people's needs and experiences. It critiques the policy path dependency and regulatory isomorphism that favour punitive and platform-centric approaches over proactive, evidence-based, and youth-centred strategies. The chapter highlights the inefficacy of current frameworks, such as the UK's Online Safety Act 2023, that emphasize stringent platform liability while failing to address the complex causes of online harm. Drawing from youth voices and historical insights, the chapter advocates for a shift towards a holistic model based on ecological systems theory, engaging stakeholders across the child's microsystem to macrosystem in collaborative, educational, and supportive roles. Ultimately, it calls for a progressive paradigm in online safety policy that prioritizes harm reduction, digital literacy, and the active participation of young people, positioning their welfare and voices at the centre of future interventions.

Keywords Online safety policy • Platform liability • Youth-centred approach • Sunk costs • Ecological systems theory

© The Author(s), under exclusive license to Springer Nature   149
Switzerland AG 2025
A. Phippen, *Policy and Rights Challenges in Children's Online
Behaviour and Safety, 2017–2023,*
https://doi.org/10.1007/978-3-031-80286-7_7

Is it knowing when to tell someone if you're upset by something that happens online?

I am fond of using the above quote, from a 13-year-old young woman during a discussion that took place in a school over ten years ago. It was during an invited session where I had been asked to do "a talk" to year 8 pupils about online safety. However, the class was small so I said I would just have a discussion, rather than giving them a talk. In the discussion one of the young people asked what I did for work, because they did not see how someone could have a job talking to young people in schools. I explained broadly that my work examined what young people did online, and what adults can do to keep them safe. I asked them what online safety meant to them. The quote above is what one of the groups said. If young people have recognized this for well over ten years, why do policy makers keep ploughing their furrow of platform liability?

As I said in Chap. 1, during this time researching the online safety space, as new technologies come and go, as do policy makers and civil servants, one thing has remained constant. Young people want help, support, and education, not heroes or saviours. And they want support from the adults around them, and they do not expect engineers in large companies far away from their lives.[1]

Yet, as we have demonstrated in this exploration of policy, path dependency, and isomorphism, as we have explored to try to understand why policy makers will only ever do more of the same, highlight how disconnected the policy space is to young people's needs. In 2008, the government accepted recommendations from the Byron Review (Byron, 2008) about multi-stakeholder approaches to tackling online safety, underpinned by education and stakeholders working to their strengths.

In 2012 a different government decided the best approach was to block content.

And as other nations adopted similar approaches, with equally hollow impact, isomorphism, it seemed, locked them on this path. Other nations

---

[1] I caveat this, once again, by stating clearly that industry, as a stakeholder in child online safety, clearly has a role to play and they are responsible for things like content moderation, monitoring problematic activity, and providing routes and tools for disclosure. However, that cannot prevent harm from occurring, and their role has to mesh with the practices of other stakeholders. Other stakeholder cannot simply sit back and shout "How did <company x> allow that to happen!?"

were adopting a prohibitive model and trying to look tough in bringing the tech sector in line, so anyone suggesting a more progressive approach might appear weak. And currently, there seems to be a legislative arms race to see who will "ban" smartphones for young people with most rapidity.

There's nothing wrong with the new laws per se. There is certainly some value in expecting platforms to provide evidence that they have thought about the potential harms that occur on their platforms and how they mitigate them. Which is what most already do to some extent. However, the political expectation that they can and should prevent harms from occurring, and the ideological obsession with holding platforms to account, with not end goal of what enough looks like, is doomed to fail.

As young people have told us, people cause upset online, and we can't expect private companies to single-handedly police the behaviour of people globally.

In the reactive approach to dealing with media outrage and policy direction driven by a coercive element of isomorphism which, by its nature, is driven by NGOs and media, will make use of edge cases to tackle the broader context of duty of care. And the path dependency manifest in the view that "well, this is the direction we're going in, so we better keep going" is clear to see.

It seems, when exploring stakeholder viers, that we have lost sight of why we are doing this. Rather than placing the child at the centre of any decision, by stakeholders at any level, it seems instead that if things feel too complex, or too hard, its better instead to demand "someone" does something about this. For example, schools could, and should (speaking from a regulatory point of view) train their staff to understand the issues of online harms and how to mitigate. But with no specification of what that training looks like, and who might deliver it, coupled with the low risk of an inspector asking about it, many schools simply do not, so the professionals in their setting do what every other adult around the child does— fall back on knowledge informed by media and moral panics, and bring their own moral judgements to decisions affecting young people. And the same could be said for others in the exosystem, as highlighted in the case discussed in Chap. 6. And the expectation to deliver education to young people, another statutory requirement, wanes considerably as young people move to secondary school, leaving them poorly informed about emerging online risks they are likely to experience through their teenaged years.

Far better, it seems, to ask a police officer to come in instead and tell them if they send nudes they might not be able to go to Disneyland.[2]

In conclusion, the ecosystem of child online safety remains fraught with challenges and paradoxes. Despite an expanding body of knowledge, heightened media attention, and robust policy interest, the approach to safeguarding children in the digital realm often appears misaligned with the nuanced needs and voices of young people. This book has delved into the systemic tensions and historical oversights that plague current policies, revealing a pattern of reactionary measures rather than proactive, evidence-based strategies.

The analysis underscores the critical need for a holistic, multi-stakeholder approach, as conceptualized through an adaptation of Bronfenbrenner's ecosystem. Effective online safety policy should incorporate the voices of young people and consider the interconnected roles of family, education systems, social services, and broader societal influences. Yet, current policies, exemplified by the UK's Online Safety Act 2023 and similar international legislations, often default to simplistic solutions such as platform liability and technological interventions, which fail to address the root causes of online harm. And when things go wrong, platforms are scapegoated as "they should have stopped it", rather than accepting the complexities of a connected ecosystem and the needs and responsibilities of the stakeholders.

Historical reviews, such as the Byron Review, have highlighted the importance of comprehensive, collaborative strategies involving education, awareness, and industry cooperation. And the Byron Review was released in 2008 and the government of the day agreed to implement its recommendations. However, recent debates and legislative actions suggest a persistent tendency to favour regulatory and punitive measures over these more complex, but ultimately more effective, approaches.

This book calls for a paradigm shift in how policy makers and stakeholders view and address child online safety. It advocates for moving beyond a narrow focus on preventing harm through bans and restrictions, towards empowering young people with the knowledge, resilience, and support they need to navigate the digital world safely. Only by aligning policy with the authentic needs and voices of young people can we hope

---

[2] This particular anecdote was told to me by a professional who had observed such an assembly and then when they asked a year 8 pupil what they had learned from it, the pupil said, "If I send a dick pic I won't be able to go to Disneyland".

to create a safer, more inclusive online environment that truly protects and empowers the next generation.

The period under review witnessed significant legislative efforts aimed at enhancing online safety, most notably the UK Online Safety Act 2023 2023. This legislation was presented as a landmark in the attempt to regulate digital spaces, imposing stringent requirements on online platforms to protect users, particularly children, from harmful content. The Act's introduction of a statutory duty of care, robust age verification measures, and enhanced content moderation mechanisms reflects a comprehensive approach to mitigating online risks. However, as explored throughout this book, the practicalities of implementing such measures are fraught with challenges, including the operational and financial burdens on platforms and the complexities of balancing safety with freedom of expression and privacy rights. While the statutory duty of care mandates that online platforms take proactive steps to prevent the dissemination of illegal content, such as child sexual exploitation, terrorism, and hate speech. Platforms are also required to conduct risk assessments and put measures in place to mitigate potential risks. However, the lack of precise definitions for what constitutes "effective" content moderation and the challenges of measuring compliance present significant obstacles for platforms.

Content moderation, while essential, is not a one-size-fits-all solution. The nature of harmful content varies widely, and algorithms designed to detect and remove such content often struggle with context and nuance. Furthermore, the implementation of robust age verification measures poses its own set of challenges. While age verification is crucial to prevent children from accessing harmful content, it raises concerns about privacy and data security. Collecting and storing age-related data introduces risks, such as data breaches and misuse of personal information. Balancing the need for age verification with the protection of user privacy requires careful consideration and the development of secure, privacy-preserving technologies.

Despite these legislative advancements, the effectiveness of these measures remains questionable. The persistence of moral panics and the tendency to prioritize reactive, prohibitionist policies over proactive, evidence-based strategies underscore the cyclical nature of online safety policy. This approach often results in measures that fail to address the root causes of online harms and overlook the nuanced needs and voices of young users. The comparison with the evolving drug policy landscape, which has increasingly adopted harm reduction strategies, suggests that a similar shift towards education, awareness, and support might yield more sustainable outcomes in the realm of online safety.

The ecological system model developed during this period, based on Bronfenbrenner's Ecology of Child Development, offers a framework for understanding the multifaceted responsibilities around online safety and the importance of the interactions between different actors in a child's environment—family, schools, public services, media, and policy makers— the model underscores the importance of a holistic approach to safeguarding. Each stakeholder plays a crucial role, and their collective efforts can create a supportive ecosystem that mitigates risks while empowering young people to navigate the digital world safely.

However, this analysis also highlights significant gaps in stakeholder engagement and collaboration. The focus often remains on external regulatory measures and platform liability, with insufficient attention to the roles of families, schools, and local communities. Engaging these microsystems more effectively could lead to more nuanced and context-specific interventions that address the diverse experiences and needs of young people. Moreover, fostering a culture of digital literacy and resilience within these closer circles can complement broader regulatory efforts, ensuring that children are better equipped to handle online challenges.

Families play a critical role in shaping children's online behaviour and safety. Parents and guardians are often the first line of defence, providing guidance, setting boundaries, and monitoring their children's online activities. However, many parents feel ill-equipped to manage the complexities of the digital world, especially given the rapid pace of technological change. Providing parents with the necessary resources, education, and support to navigate these challenges is essential. This includes promoting open communication between parents and children about online risks and encouraging parents to take an active role in their children's digital lives.

Schools also have a significant part to play in promoting online safety. Educational institutions can integrate digital literacy into their curricula, teaching students about the potential risks of online interactions and how to navigate the internet safely and responsibly. Schools can also provide training for teachers to help them understand and address online safety issues, and to create a supportive environment where students feel comfortable discussing their online experiences and concerns.

Public services, including law enforcement and child protection agencies, are crucial in responding to serious online harm incidents. These agencies need to be equipped with the knowledge and tools to effectively address online risks and to support victims of online abuse. Collaboration between public services and other stakeholders, such as schools and tech companies, can enhance the overall effectiveness of online safety efforts.

Media narratives and moral panics have played a profound role in shaping public perception and policy responses to online safety. Sensationalist reporting on issues such as online grooming, cyberbullying, and exposure to harmful content often drives a reactive policy environment, where immediate, headline-grabbing measures are prioritized over thoughtful, long-term strategies. Through the early stages of this book, we have drawn parallels with historical moral panics, such as the Satanic Panic of the 1980s, to illustrate how fear and misinformation can lead to disproportionate responses and unintended consequences, and that these moral panics rarely result in improved outcomes for those that are claimed we need to protect.

The media's portrayal of online safety issues tend to focus on extreme cases and worst-case scenarios, which can create a distorted view of the prevalence and nature of online harms. While these cases are undoubtedly serious and warrant attention, they do not represent the everyday experiences of most young people online. This skewed perception can lead to policies that are overly restrictive and fail to account for the positive aspects of digital engagement, such as social connection, learning, and creativity.

Addressing this dynamic requires a shift towards more responsible and balanced media coverage, as well as greater emphasis on public education and awareness. Providing clear, evidence-based information about online risks and the effectiveness of different safety measures can help counteract fear-driven narratives and support more rational policy-making. Additionally, involving young people in these discussions and recognizing their active role as digital citizens can help bridge the gap between adultist perspectives and the realities of youth digital experiences.

The overarching theme of this book, and indeed the majority of my work over a twenty-year period, is the need for a progressive, evidence-based approach to online safety that aligns with the lived experiences and needs of young people. Moving away from punitive, prohibitionist policies towards strategies that emphasize education, empowerment, and harm reduction can create a more sustainable framework for safeguarding children online. This approach recognizes the complexity of the digital landscape and the diverse ways in which young people engage with technology.

Key to this shift is the inclusion of youth voices in policy discussions and decision-making processes. Ensuring that young people have a say in the development and implementation of online safety measures can lead to more relevant and effective interventions. Additionally, fostering partnerships between different stakeholders, from policy makers and tech companies to educators and families, can enhance the collective capacity to address online harms in a holistic and coordinated manner.

Fostering partnerships between stakeholders is also crucial for creating a cohesive and comprehensive approach to online safety. Collaboration between policy makers, tech companies, educators, and families can facilitate the sharing of knowledge, resources, and best practices. These partnerships can also help to bridge gaps in understanding and build a shared commitment to protecting young people online.

There is a need for evidence-driven, rather than ideologically driven, policy and stakeholders decision-making, not "what I reckon"—a phrase I hear for too often from professionals claiming to adopt an evidence-based approach. I heard it when discussing the influence of violent video games on young people's offline behaviour (Phippen & Street, 2022). And I was recently told in a meeting by a senior practitioner that "just because there is no evidence doesn't mean it's not happening". However, I would suggest clairvoyance is not a good foundation upon which to support young people's needs around understanding risk online.

A FUTURE?

Certainly, it is difficult to predict what the future for online safety policy and practice might be. However, reflecting upon the conclusions in the previous book on the safeguarding dystopia and reliance on technology to prevent online harms (Phippen, 2017), the reality was perhaps starker even than anticipated. While there seem to be few trends for overreaching surveillance in the home, policy has shifted to platforms implementing the dystopia at a macro level, at the instruction of governments wishing to scapegoat them for the harms that occur online. And the legislation, which previously was considering a single use case (preventing youth access to pornography) has expanded, with the same prohibitive ideology, to any form of online harm.

If I consider what these six years might hold, it seems apparent that policy will remain driven by ideology rather than evidence. Or, where evidence is used to vindicate approach, it will ignore anything that disagrees with the approach.

The writing of this book concludes at a time, in the UK, where is Online Safety Act 2023's implementation is still under consultation with the regulator. It is moving from a legislative goal to one that a regulator might implement in a practical manner that can be both adopted by those who will be regulated (predominantly large online platforms and search engines) and also enforced.

As already discussed, a potential fall-out from stronger regulation is that there will be a lot more public information about what platforms do to tackle safety issues, borne out in their risk assessments they are expected to produce, and the transparency reports they will be mandated to provide. The value of these sorts out outputs for those developing education and interventions in the microsystem has already been discussed, but it will also mean that it will be more difficult for some actors in the macrosystem to claim that platforms do nothing or do not care.

And potentially, given that the regulator is appointed to implement a political ideology on "bringing big tech billionaires to heel" or "prevent them from profiting from children's misery", and also that there is no clear definition of the end point of "doing more", there is clearly potential that a regulatory who, as is the expected role of a regulator, works with industry to ensure alignment with the statutory duties, will also attract the ire of those who wish to continue to scapegoat industry and distract for the undeniable complexities of this space. Could regulators become the next scapegoat due to their reluctance to impose "massive" fines on companies who are clearly "doing more"?

There is already rhetoric from certain media voices and political figures criticizing the regulator for not going far enough and how if they don't children will be harmed (see below). Highlighting, once again, that there is a certain motivation among some not to ensure better outcomes for young people, but to engage in high-profile political and media battles that keep their own profiles high. When a policy with no end point, other than "stop anything bad happening online" look like becomes something that needs to be regulated, it is down the regulator to make sure what is demanded is possible, and the legislation in its current form makes this challenging.

Take, for example, the previously discussed age assurance/verification to prevent young people's access to adult content. Should a platform conducting a risk assessment and put robust age assurance in place as a result then be "held to account" if a young person bypasses this verification with privacy-enhancing tools or using someone else's verification token? And if the regulator takes the, quite correct, view that the platform has demonstrated due diligence and, given the lack of perfection in age assurance, and the roles of other stakeholders in bypassing such approaches, therefore, cannot be accountable should a determined young person achieve a bypass, might they equally become part of the more toxic elements of the ecosystem target for criticism for not caring about children? Might the locus of blame shift from the platform ("do more") to the regulator ("you're letting them get away with it!").

Writing a book like this is hard because things are always moving. Will there ever be a case for writing a book that says "Online safety used to be hard but its great now"? There is no end point, and it would seem that policy makers and NGOs, given they have not defined what "doing enough" looks like, will never take the view that the policy has reached its end goal. Because there is no end goal other than stop online harms. Which, as young people surveyed and explored in Chap. 5 very clearly tell us, are caused, predominantly, by people.

As the writing of this book was coming to an end, during the UK general election campaign 2024, the Molly Rose Foundation,[3] whose goal is stated to be suicide prevention, released a manifesto[4] calling for the next government to bring in a new Online Safety Act 2023, because the current one is not strong enough:

> Molly Rose Foundation is calling for the next Government to commit to five transformative policies that, taken together, would decisively protect young people from preventable harm and bring about a step change in their online safety and well-being.
>
> We are calling on the next Government to:
> 1 Introduce a new Online Safety Act 2023 to strengthen regulatory protections and focus the regime on achieving measurable harm reduction.
> 2 Take bold moves to ensure transparency and accountability from Big Tech, including a new duty of regulatory candour, and new measures to make companies report on user exposure to online harms in their corporate accounts.
> 3 Make the polluter pay, with a one-off harm reduction windfall tax that ensures tech companies no longer profit from harm while passing on the costs of their business model to children, families and society.

---

[3] https://mollyrosefoundation.org/
[4] http://mollyrosefoundation.org/wp-content/uploads/2024/05/MRF-Manifesto.pdf

4 Commit to a new statutory Code for app stores and operating systems, ensuring that more of the tech ecosystem has legal responsibilities to protect children and support parents.

5 Invest in mental health support and prevention schemes to ensure children and young adults get the support they need to address the risks and impacts of technology-facilitated harm.

As discussed throughout this book, at the time of writing, the Online Safety Act 2023 2023 is being turned into regulatory practice by OFCOM, the media regulator. How can anyone confidently claim that the act needs to be strengthened when its strength has not been tested. The rest of the rhetoric in the statement equally feeds into the scapegoating narrative, with little focused anywhere but platforms (bizarrely referred to as "the polluter") except for point five.

Similarly, in the political arena, the politicians want to remain tough of platforms, and in the Labour Manifesto for the 2024 election (which they went on to win).[5]

> Children and young people face significant harm online, with inappropriate content too easily available at their fingertips on a smartphone. We have seen an increase in extreme misogynistic content online driving a culture of violence against women. Labour will build on the Online Safety Act 2023, bringing forward provisions as quickly as possible, and explore further measures to keep everyone safe online, particularly when using social media. We will also give coroners more powers to access information held by technology companies after a child's death.

Even though the current Online Safety Act 2023 remains largely untested. How do they know the current legislation will not help keep everyone safe online? And if they are confident it will not; why was it not challenged during its long and winding passage through parliament?

Particularly significant, however, is a further statement in the manifesto:

> Regulators are currently ill-equipped to deal with the dramatic development of new technologies, which often cut across traditional industries and sectors. Labour will create a new Regulatory Innovation Office, bringing together existing functions across government. This office will help

---

[5] https://labour.org.uk/wp-content/uploads/2024/06/Change-Labour-Party-Manifesto-2024-large-print.pdf

regulators update regulation, speed up approval timelines, and co-ordinate issues that span existing boundaries. Labour will ensure the safe development and use of AI models by introducing binding regulation on the handful of companies developing the most powerful AI models and by banning the creation of sexually explicit deepfakes.

The new government, it seems, wants to regulate the regulators. Which does suggest that they feel regulators, at present, will not fit in with the political narrative.

So, given the analysis conducted in this book, and looking across the broad range of research I have done in this area, here are some predictions I will return to in the next volume:

- More calls to "strengthen" the online safety act. By strengthen that means further scapegoat industry for failing to stop whichever new harm emerges from a media story.
- The regulator whose roadmap to implementing the regulatory needs of the online safety act will become increasingly criticized by other stakeholders who have not read the codes of practice for failing to "hold platforms to account" and letting them off the hook" for failing to prevent online harms, even though, on the evidence presented to the regulator platforms are doing more than most people are willing to accept. They will become the second online harms scapegoat.
- Industry will continue to be told to "do more", without defining the extent of "more", only to be told it's not enough.
- Certain NGOs will continue to fuel moral panics because their business model is based on there being a significant concern for young people and an ideology that only they can solve it.
- Schools will still fail to deliver the sort of education young people are calling for and instead will fall back on popular prohibitive messages in primary school and these almost non-existent coverage in secondary settings.
- Politicians will still think being seen to be tough on platforms gets them good media coverage and reflects that they do not really have sufficient understanding of the complexities of keeping children safe online or the fact that technology alone cannot solve it. And they will continue to ignore progressive public health or education policy that might go some way to fixing the ecosystem, because that is too hard and does not fit in with political cycles.

- And young people will still call for better education and for those around them to understand the issues they face better and provide more effective support, and not call for big tech billionaires to be brought to heel. And they will be routinely ignored because "we" know better.

This may seem like a pessimistic view. However, I would prefer to regard it as a pragmatic one. Even though we have had close to twenty years of policy discussions around online safety, it is still in its infancy compared to other areas of prohibitive social policy (such as the failed "War on Drugs"—Gray, 2010). With this in mind and reflecting upon the last twelve years as I have in the two volumes of this analysis, it is fair to suggest that without a rapid change in direction, things are likely to get worse before they get better.

A Personal Reflection

On a personal level, writing this book has been something of a cathartic experience, but not one without significant annoyance. Towards the end of the first volume I raised concerns about the impact of technological intervention on young people's rights and questioned whether these dystopian interventions would actually result in the intended goal, which is, we are told, to ensure young people can go online without risk of harm.

Certainly, I am not the only academic voice who questions the validity of prohibitive policy, and I have referenced the work of excellent progressive voices in writing this book. There is a growing consensus (and it is no coincidence that all these scholars engage in qualitative research directly with young people) that this single stakeholder model of accountability is failing and education and progressive, harm reduction focused, response professionals are far more important than issuing fines to global platforms.

When conducting the policy and legal analysis, exploring datasets and reading political and media debates, it is difficult to remain entirely rational and objective because it is clear how broken the ecosystem is.

During the writing of this book, speaking to the young woman, whose case I explored in detailed in Chap. 6, brought home in a very personal way how vulnerable young people can be utterly let down by systems that are staffed by professionals who do not understand the issues, are "trained" by media narratives, who project their own moral biases onto safeguarding decisions and, bluntly, are overworked and look for the lowest effort "solution" to the issue in front of them. In the young woman's case, many adults let her down, because it was easy to dismiss her behaviour as criminal, and divert, which meant "it wasn't really too serious for her", rather than dealing with the far more complex issues in supporting a young person who was clearly groomed, whose views were ignored by the systems would add to an already overstretched workload for the professionals and one that potentially left an abuser free to abuse further.

In the last few weeks, a couple of things reminded me of how far we still need to come.

In a recent panel I was invited to speak on, there was a discussion of emerging legislation around online safety and children's privacy. One participant spoke of how "a child having a smartphone is like having a loaded gun", while another said, "we have to legislate because there is proof that children are addicted to smartphones".[6] These were (very) senior people, one from an NGO and another a regulator, whose rhetoric was far more about emotion than it was about rational discussion.

As a somewhat bizarre aside (although as I draw this book to a close this seems appropriate in a reflective section), I recently had to visit the minor injuries unit at my local hospital after a disagreement with a razor blade. As is typical in these situations one of the medical practitioners asked of what I was a professor. When I explained a little detail of my job and work (while they worked on my damaged finger), they agreed with the importance of the need for this sort of thing and then stated, "My son is 25 and he spends all day in his room playing Fortnite, I think they should ban it".

It seems, wherever I go I meet people who think online technology should be banned. It is far rarer to meet someone who talks about the need for better education/mental health services/reporting routes on platforms.

Talking further with the practitioner, I did ask whether there might be other issues affecting her son (such as unemployment, living in an extremely deprived part of the country, and mental health issues) and when we explore this, she agreed things might be more complex than just banning a particular game. She went on to say the most upsetting aspect

---

[6] I have not covered much on the addiction narratives around smartphones aside from the Haidt book. Suffice to say there are many publications and little consensus, reflecting the challenges in understanding peer-reviewed literature among policy makers, who are more likely to explore research that aligns with their own confirmation biases.

to her was hearing the language used when he is playing these games. I suggested you heard similar language on the touchline at local football matches. She agreed and said she had observed that at their local football club. As we departed, my finger back to something resembling a finger, she said she had enjoyed our chat and it had helped her see things differently.

It's amazing what a little discussion will achieve. Which is why it is so frustrating to see the political classes pursuing their ideological obsession and sunk costs, and refusing to engage in conversations that suggest there might be a better way.

Finally, in a recent stakeholder workshop, which was a coming together of several progressive voices in the sector to discuss how we might achieve better outcomes for children, a senior industry practitioner talks about some tools they had co-created with young people. He was saying how much he learned from listening to the young people.

It is something I hear a lot.

I can remember many years ago attending a class in a local school for a discussion with young people about online safety. The head of the school asked if she could sit in on the session. Once the students had got over the discomfort of the head being sat there (none of them had spoken to her before), they were as open and honest as most of the groups of young people I have spoken to and eventually they joined in with the discussion and asked questions while being honest about her own ignorance of many of the issues the young people were raising. After the session had finished, she thanked me and said how much she had learned "by listening to young people".

It is amazing what happens when we listen to young people.

REFERENCES

Bryon Review. (2008). *Safer children in a digital world: The report of the Bryon review*. Department for Children, Schools and Families.

Gray, J. (2010). *Why our drug laws have failed: A judicial indictment of war on drugs*. Temple University Press.

Phippen, A. (2017). *Children's online behaviour and safety: Policy and rights challenges*. Springer.

Phippen, A., & Street, L. (2022). *Online resilience and wellbeing in young people*. Springer.

Index[1]

---

[1] Note: Page numbers followed by 'n' refer to notes.

The manufacturer's authorised representative in the EU is Springer
Nature Customer Service Centre GmbH, Europaplatz 3, 69115 Heidelberg,
Germany. If you have any concerns regarding our products, please
contact ProductSafety@springernature.com

Printed and bound by CPI Group (UK) Ltd, Croydon, CR0 4YY

29/04/2026

02099538-0006